Instructor's Resource Manual

THE ART OF THE ESSAY

Instructor's Resource Manual

THE ART OF THE ESSAY

Lydia Fakundiny
Department of English
Cornell University

HOUGHTON MIFFLIN COMPANY   BOSTON

Dallas   Geneva, Illinois   Palo Alto   Princeton, New Jersey

Copyright © 1991 by Houghton Mifflin Company. All rights reserved.

Permission is hereby granted to teachers to reprint or photocopy this work or portions thereof in classroom quantities for use in their classes with accompanying Houghton Mifflin material, provided each copy made shows the copyright notice. Such copies may not be sold and further distribution is expressly prohibited. Except as authorized above, prior written permission must be obtained from Houghton Mifflin Company to reproduce or transmit this work or portions thereof in any other form or by any other electronic or mechanical means, including any information storage or retrieval system, unless expressly permitted by federal copyright law. Address inquiries to College Permissions, Houghton Mifflin Company, One Beacon Street, Boston, MA 02108.

Printed in the U.S.A.

ISBN: 0-395-57115-4

ABCDEFGHIJ-CS-99876543210

Contents

Preface

This manual is not a prescription for teaching the essay; nor, strictly, does it purport to be a guide to teaching. As the pedagogic extension of *The Art of the Essay* it offers some paradigms of experience in the classroom: it reports how one teacher tries to engage students in the reading and writing of essays with the hope of heightening their awareness of the task along with their expectations of themselves.

Part I, "Thinking About Essays," illustrates an approach to studying texts through chains of questions that may be asked of published pieces and student writing alike. While specifically intended for class discussion, these questions can and do establish analytic models for the student as reader-critic and as working essayist.

Part II, "Two Narratives of Teaching," sketches out two different courses on the essay that I have worked up over roughly the last decade. Both combine reading and writing; both stress the student's dual responsibility as critic and as essayist; both reach toward the production of essays that demonstrate a complex grasp of the genre, of the craft essential to its practice, and of the art that may, if the practitioner is faithful and lucky, spring from that craft. The two courses may be taught independently of each other or as complementary halves of a yearlong sequence.

Part III, "Students as Essayists," compiles nine essays by Cornell undergraduates produced in one or another of my classes on the essay in recent years. They are in that sense proof, as it were, of this teacher's pedagogic pudding. I present them to emphasize as strongly as I know how the productive role that successful student writing can play in the classroom. The nine are here partly by chance (picked from whatever manuscripts happened to have accumulated in my files) and partly by choice, specifically the good judgment and taste of David Levine, a member of English 389 in the fall term of 1989. I am grateful to David for agreeing to introduce those pieces and for collaborating with me in the perhaps risky venture of showing what can come of all this preoccupation with the essay.

L.F.

PART I

Thinking About Essays

Our readiest terminology for analyzing nonfiction prose—the language of "introduction," "thesis," "body," "topic sentence," "conclusion," and so on—is, in my experience, the least useful for thinking critically and productively about essays. Most essays simply don't adhere, or adhere very imperfectly, to this familiar model of exposition and argument that has become so fundamental to the teaching of composition and the classroom analysis of associated readings. Take up a poem, and people start talking in one way or another about its language; take up a short story, and the focus is all on character, plot, setting, and the like; but consider a piece of nonfiction prose (especially one in a "textbook"), and the discussion turns inevitably to what the author "says" as everyone goes hunting for key formulations of the authorial message (theses, topic sentences, transitions, etc.) in all the expected places within the text. Teaching prose of the kind collected in *The Art of the Essay* becomes in part a matter of working against such structural formulas of the academic, or "school," essay, of calling into question habitual expectations about how prose discourses may be organized, and, thus, transforming both how we read essays and how we write them. Indeed, the primary challenge of teaching the essay, whether as a text to be construed (*i.e.*, read) or as one to be produced (written), seems to me to be this: coming up with a workable critical language, one sufficiently fresh, flexible, and exact to enable members of a class on the essay to describe to themselves and to others just how, and how well, any one such text does its work. To vitalize the way in which students read *and* write essays, we need to foster a new kind of attention to essayistic prose, to point them down unfamiliar, and yet to be marked, paths of inquiry.

I tend to teach mainly by posing questions and by chaining questions together in ways that impel the class forward as a community of individuals striving, in concert, to clarify how a given text manages to engage them. If this kind of class is to be a genuine inquiry—rather than, on the one hand, a guided tour whose itinerary and terminus are known to me or, on the other, a mere succession of disjunct monologues—everyone in the class, myself included, must be more than ordinarily attentive to everyone else, must expend at least as much intellectual effort listening to others as we each expend on articulating our own puzzles and insights. Everyone, in other words, must be willing to participate in something like a group conversation: people turning their minds to some shared intellectual endeavor, groping collaboratively towards clarification and understanding. The process is not a neat one. Only very rarely does it yield (and it need not become) a linear movement towards unequivocal

enlightenment; members of a class move at various paces and with varying degrees of reservation about what is going on among them. I see
my own task in such discussions as threefold: (1) to encourage attentive-
ness and dialogue, conversation rather than mere expressive interchanges
or competitive speech-making; (2) to clarify, whenever needful and op-
portune, where we collectively are and where we seem to be headed—or
simply to articulate the muddle we may be in; (3) to keep the process
moving along a chain of questions maintaining the sense of a coherent
and focussed, though perhaps very intricate, inquiry.

What follows is such a chain of questions. This is neither a record
of nor a prescription for any particular class on any given essay; rather,
I want to indicate only the possible scope and direction of discussion
about essays and to introduce a language, tentative and always subject
to adjustment, for such discussions. The questions assume as little as
possible about the genre's formal properties so that each essay may be
made to speak on its own terms. They are ordered under four headings:

BEGINNINGS: Where does this essay start?
AMPLIFICATION: How does it grow?
VOICE: Who is "there" in this essay?
CLOSURE: Where does this essay end (up)?

These headings are deliberately nonschematic, mutually nonexclusive,
forcing shifts among analytic levels and reorientations within the text
under discussion. They form a possible *sequence* of inquiry—*i.e.*, a possible order to be followed in considering a particular essay—while showing
the importance of staying mobile, of reconsidering, when necessary, the
same ground from another angle, such as going over, or back over, an
essay's opening (BEGINNINGS) *via* questions about its voice (VOICE).
Under each heading, increasingly specific questions issue from a more
general or key question, the idea being to keep elaborating the search so
that the essay's shape and the essayist's craft may emerge as fully as
possible. Hypothetically, of course, such questions might be elaborated
almost *ad infinitum,* down to the smallest detail of language, as one gets
closer and closer to the textuality of any given essay under consideration.

It must be emphasized that these questions are equally applicable to
published essays and to essays written by students. In my class, we talk
exactly the same way about, ask the same questions of, and make the
same demands upon a manuscript turned in by a member of the class
and a selection in one of our books. That is to say, the implied critical
stance of the questions that follow combines *analytical* and *interpretive*
processes (ordinarily applied to texts we read in books) with *evaluative*
processes (usually applied to the texts students write). I have found that
students both read and write much better, more discerningly and more
maturely, when the texts they produce are judged by the same standards

and considered in the same light as the texts they construe out of books. Treating a student essay as one would an essay in a book identifies the former's virtues as rapidly as it exposes flaws; this makes the class critique of papers truly productive and the work of "revision" a central part of the writer's enterprise. Treating a seemingly immovable published text as verbal craft to be studied, assessed, and savored turns the printed page into the freshly apprehensible traces of a particular writer's passage through the world of words; this makes "literature" as vital, as much a proof of personal endeavor, as the paper turned in by one's neighbor, even perhaps as the one that just came off one's own uncertain production line.

BEGINNINGS

Where does this essay start?

(1) Where in the *world of discourse* are we? How does this essay open? What goes on in the first paragraph or two? What kind of discoursive material is this? Is it story, description, exposition, polemic?

- If story, in what narrative frame (when, where, who, what) does the essay's opening situate the reader?
- If description, what sensory experiences (visual, aural, tactile, olfactory, gustatory) are being rendered and with what impact?
- If exposition, what topic (notion, process, issue, concern, idea) is being addressed by what means (explanation, definition, analysis)?
- If polemic, what stand is being taken about what, what adversarial posture adopted against what or whom, what position or action advocated or defended?

(2) Where in the *world of human experience* are we? In other words, what seems to have set this writer writing?

- What is he or she responding to or noticing in the world?
- What is he or she trying to do—e.g., share something, get hold of something, make sense of something, come to terms with something, give voice to something? In other words, from what impetus or nexus of feeling does this material seem to arise?
- Is this slight, even trivial, material for this writer? Is it significant, problematic, grave, explosive? How can we tell? Where in the language (the diction and syntax) can we locate the writer's motive, stance, attitude? (See more under VOICE.) How certain can we be of our judgments at this point in the essay?

AMPLIFICATION

How does this essay grow?

How does it *enlarge* (*i.e.*, elaborate, develop, complicate) and *build* (*i.e.*, structure) the topic addressed, broached, or implied at the outset? That is, *where* does the essay go from its starting point, and *how* does it keep going?

(1) Can we mark off major breaks, divisions, shifts, and links of thought along the essay's path of elaboration?

— How do paragraph divisions work in this process of amplification? Do the beginnings and endings of paragraphs signal distinct stages of thought (structural paragraphing), or are they designed primarily to draw the reader along and keep him or her engaged in the flow of the discourse (rhetorical paragraphing)?

— Does the essay anywhere pause, dawdle, dilate some idea unexpectedly, digress, or wander? Where and over what? Are these dilations and/or digressions merely distracting, and if so, from what do they distract? If not, what justifies their presence in the essay? That is, how does the digression contribute, if it does, to the structure and overall effect of the essay?

(2) Working from Edward Hoagland's claim (*The Art of the Essay*, p. 691) that an essay, however unconventionally formed, "somewhere contains a point which is its center," we might ask: what is the "center" of this essay we are discussing?

— What is its conceptual heart as a discourse (whether expressed in so many words or largely implied)? If there is no "thesis" as such (*i.e.*, explicit formulation of the "center"), what is the essay's "theme," to use a term from fiction?

— Can we locate this center? Is it to be found somewhere in the essay's opening, to be specified and elaborated in what follows? Or does the essay move and gather toward this center somewhere near the end? Or is the "point" of the essay literally somewhere *at* the center, the whole discourse enlarging around it, somewhat as a pearl grows around a granule of sand?

— Is this center to be located in any single sentence, or run of sentences, or in a loosely related string of sentences scattered across the discourse? If not, how *do* we go about formulating a theme (implicit, nonlocalized key idea) for this essay? If we can't arrive at such a formulation, why not? Does it matter?

(3) What modes of discourse move the essay forward?

— If story, is this, broadly speaking, *recollective* narrative (personal reminiscence driven by memory) or *historical* narrative (the account of public events, processes, etc., based on communal sources including written records)?

— If description, to what senses does this language appeal (sight, touch, hearing, smell, taste)? Is the language mainly *evocative* (recreating sensory experience) or *affective* (generating mood or atmosphere)? Is the description tied to place?

— If exposition, does the discourse function mainly to *clarify* (explain, analyze, define) or to *reflect* (ruminate, interpret, speculate, evaluate, synthesize)?

— If polemic, does the argument rely mainly on *logical* devices (deduction and induction, giving reasons, moving from cause to effect, from purpose to result) or on *rhetorical means* (appeals to feeling, value, and taste through semantic coloring and shifting, analogies, *ad hominem* addresses, etc.)?

— Does any one discursive mode predominate in this essay? *I.e.,* is the essay shaped mainly by storytelling, by evoking the sensory world, by the impetus to explain and understand, or by the urge to sway, compel, and move? What secondary modes are intertwined with this dominant mode of discourse and with what effect on the pace and texture of amplification? For example, if the essay is primarily intent on clarifying and explaining, what effect do narrative excursions have on the expository process? Do they function strictly as "examples" (*i.e.,* conceptual specification)?

(4) How might we describe the *pattern* of amplification—the structuring of the elaboration—in this essay?

— Does the essay unfold in linear fashion, piece by piece, stage by stage? Or does the thought grow by ramification, somewhat like the branches of a tree from a central trunk? Does the essay circle back over itself, revisiting ideas again and again in a spiral? Does the thought build layer by layer? (Another way of viewing this last pattern is under the image of rumination or "chewing the cud," *i.e.,* passing the topic or problem under consideration through a multiple, repeated digestive process). Does the thought move outward from some point, widening and extending its scope in a sort of ripple effect?

— Is the essay organized along some *physical trajectory*—a walk, search, journey, ramble? (See, *e.g.,* Addison's "The Tombs at Westminster Abbey," Dickens's "Night Walks," Hawthorne's "Footsteps on the Sea-shore," Walker's "Looking for Zora," McClane's "Walls: A Journey to Auburn.")

— Is the essay focussed by means of a *controlling image* (perhaps an initial image, as in Emerson's "Illusions" and Rhodes's "The Death of the Everglades") or by a *controlling metaphor* (Donne's "The Physician is Sent For," Eiseley's "The Winter of Man")?

— Is it structured by some pattern of *conceptual contrasts* (*e.g.,* Stevenson's "Apology for Idlers," Ozick's "The Riddle of the Ordinary," Lawrence's "Whistling of Birds") or *rhetorical contrast* (McClane's "Walls: A Journey to Auburn" and Rhodes's "The Death of the Everglades")?

— Is the essay built upon a story (*e.g.,* Macaulay's "The Royal Society of Literature," Twain's "Corn-Pone Opinions," Montaigne's "Of Practice")?

(5) Emerson writes somewhere that "good writing is a kind of skating that carries off the performer where he would not go."

— Can we spot the essay that takes "the performer" to unexpected terrain, as against the essay that follows a preconceived map?

— How can we distinguish where an author "would go" from where he or she "would not go" but did? In other words, how can we tell what "the performer" intended in an essay and where and how he or she got carried off?

— How do we evaluate the effect of the author's being carried off? In other words, can we distinguish, *in the language of an essay,* between a failed intention—an author meaning to go somewhere and not making it—and a successful performance in Emerson's terms, where the writer discovers, in the process of writing, something better, more interesting, than what he or she had in mind at the outset?

— How do we spot the residue of abandoned intentions in an essay and what do we do with this residue as writers?

VOICE

Who is "there" in this essay?

What kind of "human voice"—to use Hoagland's phrase (*The Art of the Essay,* p. 691)—is "talking" here? What is the quality of mind and feeling, the stance towards self and world, that we catch in this essay as we read? How is the "voice" inscribed in the language, the discoursive texture and style of the essay?

(1) Thoreau writes in *Walden* that "it is . . . always the first person that is speaking." Is the first person readily discernible in the essay

under discussion, or is it recessive? How much in the linguistic foreground is the essayistic self?

— How prominent are forms of the first-person pronoun (I, my, mine), and in what contexts do they appear?
— Does the essayist's "I" function explicitly as the subject of the discourse, *i.e.*, of reminiscence and/or speculation? In other words, is this an "I" thinking about itself or an "I" directed primarily outward towards other things? Do the kind and degree of self-preoccupation create intimacy or distance?

(2) What does this "I" know? Value? Notice? Care about? What, in Hazlitt's words, is this essayist's "stock of ideas" ("On Going a Journey")? (One might ask, for instance, what does the Dillard of "Life on the Rocks" know, value, notice, care about? The Steiner of "A Kind of Survivor"? The Huxley of "Hyperion to a Satyr"? The Sanders of "Doing Time in the Thirteenth Chair"? The Blackwood of "Portrait of a Beatnik"?)

— What do we learn from the essay under discussion about the writer's intellectual, experiential, and emotional reach? What kinds of knowledge, perceptions, observations, insights, attitudes, feelings, memories does this essayist's mind seem to be stocked with? What, in other words, are the dimensions and attributes of this writer's sensibility?
— What is this essayist's range of reference, both explicit (what is discussed) and implicit (in the kinds of images and metaphors that characterize the discourse)?
— What areas of ignorance or of insensitivity does this writer admit and/or inadvertently betray? Where are the blind spots in this "I"?

(3) What is this essayist's relationship to his or her material (*i.e.*, subject matter)? Where does he or she stand in relation to it in terms of time and space (far removed, close, partly removed, etc.)? What present concerns seem to give rise to the calling up of temporarily and/or spatially distant material?

— How charged (*i.e.*, emotionally significant and complex) is this material for this author? What is his or her emotional distance from it? How does this author manage his or her feelings about the material—with candor, self-indulgence, restraint, aloofness, detachment, fervor? (See also (6): ironic voices.)
— What do particular features of style suggest about the essayist's relationship to the material and, more broadly, about his or her experience of being in the world? For instance, inasmuch as a

highly connected (hypotactic) syntax tends to express and emphasize the urge to understand and explain what is at issue, and inasmuch as the suppression of connections (asyndeton and parataxis) assumes and acknowledges, even dramatizes, the difficulty (perhaps futility) of making the very connections essential to explanatory discourse, what do the various ways of making or suppressing connections within and among sentences suggest about this writer's relationship to the material (and to the audience)? How might a highly metaphoric style portray the essayist's processing of experience and the world he or she inhabits? What might a style shorn of figurative language suggest about a writer's experience and about his or her relationship to language?

(4) What relationship does the voice in a given essay posit between writer and reader? What kind and degree of distance are created by the character of the discourse (*i.e.*, discursive mode) and by the essay's style?

— Does an essayist's intimacy with the reader depend on the prominence of first-person pronouns? What other indices are there of the degree of distance the essayist puts between himself or herself and the reader? How do the several modes of discourse (narrative, descriptive, expository, argumentative) adjust and modulate the distance between writer and reader? Do some kinds of discoursing tend to bring writer and reader closer to each other? Do some tend to distance? Are narrative and descriptive discourses inherently more intimate than exposition and argument? Why do we tend to regard reminiscence (usually narrative and descriptive) as more intimate, more personal, than explanation and argument? Need we do so?

— Does the "I" of the essay address the reader directly? If not, does anything in the essay suggest the writer's acknowledgment/ awareness of the reader's presence? In what spirit are these addresses and/or acknowledgments offered?

— Can some model of human relationship (*e.g.*, friend-friend, student-teacher, parent-child, boss-employee, colleague-colleague, sisterhood, brotherhood) serve to describe the relationship between reader and writer created by the "I" of the essay?

(5) What is the writer's attitude to himself or herself in the essay? Robert Frost's famous utterance that "style is the way the man takes himself" may be transposed thus: "tone is the way the man takes himself" (tone being lodged in language, that is, in style). How, we might ask, does the "I" of the essay regard itself, either explicitly, by way of actual self-reference, or implicitly, by how the "I" presents itself to the

reader in the progress of the discourse? (How, for instance, does Addison "take himself" in "The Tombs at Westminster Abbey"? How does Theroux in "Cowardice" take himself? How does Welty in "A Sweet Devouring" take indiscriminate childhood self? How does Hurston take her "colored" self? How does Baker take his youthfully romantic and chauvinistic self? How does Stevenson take his "idling" self? His "apologetic" self? How does the Johnson of *Rambler* No. 146 take his authorial self? How does Woolf in "The Death of the Moth" take her human mortal self? How does Didion in "On Mortality" take her moralist self?) How, in other words, do given essayists regard themselves in their works, and how does the language of their essays create that attitude towards and valuation of self?

(6) How do we detect and interpret, construe, unravel, ironic voices?

— How do we decide, for instance, that Swift's "A Modest Proposal" is not to be adopted in earnest? That Fielding's "Essay on Nothing" is not to be read as a pretentiously vapid treatise but as a witty spoof on pretentiousness and vapidity? That Lamb's "The Convalescent" is not a piece of self-aggrandizement but a piece of self-deflation? That Beerbohm's "A Relic" is not a memoir of youthful genius but a reflection of youthful grandiosity and self-delusion? That Welty's "A Sweet Devouring" is not a naive report of a child's reading habits but a meditation on the formation of taste? That Baker's "The Flag" is not a manifesto of male chauvinist superpatriotism but a provocative critique of that posture?
— How do we differentiate among these many kinds and degrees of irony? What is the attitude of any one such ironic voice to the essay's subject matter, the reader, the self?
— When does ironic language move into fiction; the ironic voice become a "mask" or anti-self? How do such anti-selves manage nonetheless to be vehicles of truthfulness?
— How does ironic language control, deflect, suppress, modify, side-step feeling (*e.g.*, rage, indignation, shame, irritation, fear, love, hate)? When does irony become an escape from feeling or from the truth of experience? Or what does the ironic voice conceal, and to what end?
— How might a given ironic essay be rewritten nonironically (*i.e.*, avoiding all indirection, meeting ideas and feeling head-on)? What might be learned from such an exercise of rhetorical translation?

CLOSURE

Where does this essay end (up)?

Does it bring its subject to resolution, to a point of completion? Or does it leave off indeterminately, without closing the problems and questions raised? In other words, what is finished when the essay ends? What is left unfinished?

(1) What is in the last paragraph or two?

— What kind of discoursive material is this? (See questions in section (1) of BEGINNINGS.)
— Does the essayist seem at pains to pull together, finish out, the essay's theme? Does he or she take hold of the topic in some purposive way at the end, to re-focus it, to squeeze the last drop of meaning out of it, to reach some "conclusion" about it?
— If the essay closes with a clear resolution of its material, is this resolution convincing, *i.e.*, large enough and complex enough to accommodate the range of issues raised within the essay? Is the resolution too neat, too eager? What kinds of doubts, if any, does it raise about the essayist's grasp of the material and of his or her control of the craft of writing essays?
— If the essay leaves off either abruptly, or uncertainly, or tentatively, or suggestively (rather than roundly, resoundingly, and securely), does this finish seem consonant with the direction of the essay's amplification and with the voice?

(2) Where does the essayist end up in relation to the material? Where is he or she left in the world of human experience (using the word roughly as Porter does in "St. Augustine and the Bullfight")?

— What perspective does the ending create on the essayist's project, the motives that set him or her writing? How, in other words, does the last paragraph to two seem to assess the particular project of essaying that now draws to a close? Does the "I" seem satisfied with where the essay has taken him or her? Uncertain? Troubled? Resigned? Heartened? Inspired?
— Has this essayist discovered, learned, figured out something by the end of the essay? Made up his or her mind about anything? Has the essay—the writing of it—made a difference?

A NOTE ABOUT STYLE

In this material I have included occasional questions on style largely as a reminder that such questions may be addressed at any point in the discussion of an essay. Indeed, issues of style arise—and should arise—everywhere the more closely one looks at a text, whether a published essay or one created by a member of the class. For style is, after all, not a formal overlay of a discourse but its very matrix. Style is and must be a part of the work from the beginning; the continuum of composing, rewriting, and editing is to be seen as the ever more closely and finely controlled process of honing language in harmony with purpose, suiting the style *to* the purpose, and discovering the purpose *in* the style: shaping the thought in and by the word. Questions about motive and voice, therefore, about amplification and discoursive texture (the particular weave of discoursive modes in an essay), as well as about "meaning" of all sorts, turn in the practical critiques of close reading upon matters of word choice and sentence formation. Recurrent attention to style reorients the critique from consideration of seemingly disembodied "ideas" and "thoughts" to the words and sentences construed from the page before us, the language by and in which these ideas and thoughts live.

On addressing questions of style analytically and thus acquiring habits of stylistic attention and analysis, see *The Art of the Essay,* pp. 713–740. On fostering stylistic awareness in the classroom and, in particular, promoting a sense of style as grounded in one's motives and sensibilities as an essayist, see the segment on imitation in Narrative B ("Two Narratives of Teaching," Part II of this manual).

PART II

Two Narratives of Teaching

BACKGROUND

"The Art of the Essay" (English 388 in the fall, 389 in the spring term) has been a standard part of the English curriculum at Cornell for many years. Alongside "Narrative Writing," "Verse Writing," "Autobiography," and, most recently, critical writing about literature, "The Art of the Essay" is offered as an upper level seminar for undergraduates who have satisfied the university's two-semester writing requirement. More often than not, students interested in it have also done writing at the 200 level, either "expository" or "creative," sometimes both. Like its companion courses at the same level, "The Art of the Essay" has no formal prerequisites; it simply asks that students, whatever their majors or professional ambitions, "have done well in" previous writing classes. Various members of the department have taught this course, each of us very much in his or her own fashion; the instructor's freedom to design the course as he or she pleases is one of its great strengths and attractions from year to year. I have taught 388/389 on and off since 1981; *The Art of the Essay* is both the fruit of that teaching and the answer to my own need for a versatile text. In both versions of the course (henceforth "A" and "B") as I teach it, reading and writing are fully integrated, interdependent, and mutually productive.

Admission to the class is on the basis of writing samples submitted to me in advance; equally important is the student's willing commitment to the course and its requirements as explained in the first class meeting. In the writing samples (two or three recent papers in prose, including fiction if available), I look for a level of literacy appropriate to writing at the college level:

— Good control of syntax and diction (no, or only very slight, "errors")
— Competent reasoning within paragraphs, along with some sense of amplitude and fluency (something beyond the telegraphic newspaper paragraph)
— The ability to focus a problem and work it out coherently over several pages (four to five at a minimum)
— Signs of "promise," however rudimentary or undisciplined (*e.g.*, verbal playfulness, syntactic daring, analytical or imaginative complexity)

I look, in other words, for competence in written English of a fairly conventional kind, along with hints that the writer somehow relishes the solitary business of doing things with words on the page. I do not admit students with "writing problems"; such students are usually referred to suitable courses at the 200 level.

The first class meeting is an opportunity for the fifteen individuals so selected to decide whether the course is for them, whether they are prepared to undertake the particular kinds of responsibilities it imposes. I emphasize that "The Art of the Essay" both demands and attempts to foster a high degree of self-motivation, self-reliance, and self-discipline. It calls for:

— A more than casual interest in reading and writing, including the willingness to work at writing on a regular (preferably a daily) basis and thus to create the conditions for cultivating the craft of writing as a discipline

— A readiness to participate in a *community* of readers and writers, individuals involved in a common enterprise, each of whom is prepared to share his or her work with others in the class and to take the work of others as seriously as his or her own, *i.e.,* to be both a writer and a critic

I establish and clarify the following *essential procedures*:

— Everyone is expected to attend all classes and to arrive in class on time. Students whose schedules (or temperaments) might prevent them from meeting this basic condition of the course are discouraged from enrolling in it, however talented they may seem.

— No grades are assigned to individual papers as they come in; an "evaluation" in this course means a critique (written and/or oral). Written critiques may run from a paragraph to a page or more.

— Writing "deadlines" are understood as commitments between individual writers and *the class as a whole* (rather than the instructor). Because student essays are at the center of the course, papers must come in on a *regular* basis, as promised and/or prearranged; otherwise, there can be no class, no ongoing collective enterprise.

— Papers must be brought to class in duplicate (triplicate if the writer expects to be reading aloud the day the essay comes in). One copy goes to me, one to a member of the class willing to write a second critique and, if feasible, to confer with the writer at a mutually convenient time outside of class. Students are responsible for arranging such second readings with their classmates and for providing critiques promptly (by the next class meeting, if possible). Inasmuch as written critiques become a part of the *critic's* final portfolio, that person should retain a copy of his or her critique.

— Writers should be prepared to read their work aloud (by prearrangement with me). If all goes well, everyone ends up reading twice per semester, more often if time permits and the work merits more frequent exposure. Being prepared to read aloud means not only having a good typescript in hand but also putting some time and thought into the reading as a *performance*. Students are urged to practice reading aloud with each other (outside of class) and to consult with me for additional practice if they feel uneasy about this key aspect of their classwork. Many very good writers may never have thought of their writing as something *heard* and need practice reading aloud to do justice (and in some instances, to improve) their prose.

— I discourage the submission (either to me or to others) of "drafts" of papers, *i.e.,* compositions in the rough. A first principle of the course is that each writer is expected at all times to turn in his or her *best* work for the scrutiny of others; this means taking a piece of writing as far as possible on one's own, to achieve what feels, at least for the time being, like a stable, fully amplified, stylistically polished text and to come to class with a clean, closely proofread manuscript.

— The corollary of this is that all writing is considered to be work in progress subject to continuing revisions right up until the last day of the term. (In practice, most students will rework about two-thirds of their essays two to four times, with whatever intervening critiques they can get from me and others.)

— The final portfolio is due on the last day of classes and should contain all versions of every essay the student has attempted during the term (as well as any other writing, including imitations and written critiques of others' work). The best—*i.e.,* most nearly finished and polished—versions go to the front of the portfolio and should represent a significant proportion of the whole. An index noting the order of manuscripts in the portfolio and the status of each introduces the work. The course grade is based, in the main, on the student's best work, with some weight given to the quality of earlier written versions and to the student's performance as a critic.

NARRATIVE A

I originally conceived of "The Art of the Essay" as a practical exploration, through reading and writing personal essays, of the notion of "voice," using that term to designate the "I" of a given essay as constructed by its language. The idea was to investigate and wrestle with the relationship between this verbally crafted "I"—this essayistic voice —and what one experiences in ordinary life as one's "self." I wanted my students to move beyond two opposing and, in different ways, suspect (also, in my opinion, dangerous) notions of writing: (1) that writing is self-expression pure and simple, the portrayal in words for the benefit of others of a preformed, stable self that has "something to say" and knows what that something is, a linguistic vehicle needed only for transporting inner realities ("thoughts") out into the world of social, verbally negotiated interactions; and (2) that writing is a kind of masquerade or camouflage with ulterior motives, the putting on of an act for the sake of some audience having to be manipulated for the writer's own ends, the striking of postures calculated to achieve compliance of one sort or another with the writer's own view of things. The first of these notions (that writing is the "expression" of a fully formed self) seems to most students natural and obvious, reinforced as it is by pedagogies that urge the writer to "find" (as thought it was already "there") his or her "own" or "real" voice; the second (that writing is a species of calculated coercion) appears more and more to be regarded as a sophisticated necessity of living in the world as it is today. By contrast, my essay class would, I hoped, move its members toward an experience of writing as reciprocally expressive *and* constructive: the essayist both feels that he or she "has" something to say and discovers through the process of writing what that something is. Writing becomes the creation of thought and, inevitably, the occasion of the thinker's coming into being—of an "I" being formed that in some way defines and sustains the essayist's self. The construction of this "I" (voice) by way of writing necessarily posits the character of some receptive other, some second "self" qualified to listen (the "reader").

This has continued to be the operating premise of English 388, the fall (or "A") version of "The Art of the Essay" as I teach it. Working within the broad rhetorical traditions of the essay in English, I focus the course on a range of voices organized under the general rubrics "polemical" and "reflective." Polemical voices are, in various modes and to varying degrees, adversarial: the writer is impelled by some motive that places him or her in opposition to something. Polemical voices defend, attack, criticize, advocate, challenge, provoke, subvert, undercut, expose, move—any or all of these, in almost any combination and with varying degrees of emotional intensity (passion), forthrightness, and conviction. Reflective voices are generally nonadversarial, driven by motives not of self-assertion but of understanding. Reflective voices recollect, represent, evoke, sort out, analyze, define, explain, weigh, ponder, ruminate, meditate—any or all of these, in nearly any combination and to varying depths of insight. Sometimes they sound coolly cerebral, sometimes deeply nuanced with feeling. The class considers and discusses published essays in each range, both older and recent, not so much as strict models for writing but as resources for searching out their own motives and trying out their own skills as essayists. Reading and writing fall into four parts or stages (of a roughly fourteen-week term):

— Essays exploring the writer's motives (reflective)
— Apologetic essays (polemical)
— Ironic and satiric essays (polemical)
— Essays about people and places (reflective)

Motives (3 Weeks)

In the first class meeting, I read aloud the must suggestive bits from Orwell's "Why I Write" and from Didion's more recent essay by that name (see passages cited under "Essayists and Their Art," pages 699–700, *The Art of the Essay*). Students who wish to read one or both of these essays in full are referred to the library reserve shelf or to any number of paperbacks in my office, which they are welcome to peruse during my office hours. The first piece of writing, due within a week of the introductory session, is a short essay (1,000–1,200 words) exploring their own motives, attitudes, habits as writers: How does writing matter to me? What is it for in my life? How much time do I give to it? What moves me to write? How does the classroom promote and/or inhibit my impulses, goals, and *modus operandi* as a writer? Am I a writer when I'm *not* writing? How do I feel about writing? About myself as a writer? These and other such questions are meant to set off introspection of a very focussed kind: they try to get at the writing self so as to draw that self, that dimension of the student's life, into the foreground for a semester, among other such writing selves. While students are working on this first essay, I ask them to browse through our text, reading whatever snags their interest and staying on the lookout for the motives that might impel a given essay they've chosen to read. Class time (if any) goes to discussion of these browsings—what interesting essays have turned up in our book, what makes them interesting, how the motivational issue comes in, and so on. Students become acquainted with their books in this way and make their initial, undirected forays into the literary tradition to which they will shortly become contributors.

When the first essays are ready, the reading aloud begins. It takes about two weeks' worth of classes to hear from everyone, with only brief discussions as we go from one writer to the next. The paramount thing, at this point, is to hear everyone around the table speak as a writer: to hear everyone's actual voice delivering what he or she has wrought. During these weeks of reading aloud, I let students hold onto their own essays, encouraging them to rework and improve as they see fit until the date of submission (usually the final reading day). The most immediate practical consequence of these initial performances is the consolidation of the class as a writing community, a diverse group of individuals learning to know, respect, and trust each other *as* writers. These first essays serve at the same time as a stimulus to self-awareness and as a catalyst for essays to come. They often contain germs of future writing attempts, so that successive papers may take on a cohesiveness of purpose and outlook that is exciting both for individual writers and for the class as a whole. (Indeed, it was this tendency toward connections among a given student's individual essays that suggested to me the form of course B.)

If there is time to spare in this segment of the course, I like to xerox the first paragraph of every essay, pasting the paragraphs up in a running manuscript copied whole for every member of the class so that we can now look at and characterize informally all the "voices" as they succeed each other in these pages—voices created by words alone, apart from any given writer's physical speaking presence. (An occasion for introducing some of the kinds of questions posed under VOICE in Part I of this manual.) The scrutiny of these first paragraphs has proven to be a good device for opening up the complex issue of how an essay's voice relates to the writer's self.

Apologetic Essays (3 Weeks)

I launch this phase of the course not with an essay but with a reading from the canon of Western philosophy: Plato's "Apology." (I like the version in *The Collected Dialogues of Plato,* edited by Edith Hamilton and Huntington Cairns.) The distance created by studying a discourse so apparently different from the essay brings our concern as polemical writers into a sharp, yet richly suggestive, focus, moving us past the assumption that what we are about to learn to write is some kind of "argument" with a thesis and proofs and so on. We consider the character of Socrates (*i.e.,* his *ethos*) as it emerges from his situation, his account of himself, and the nature of his appeals to his accusers and jurors. What, we may ask, is at stake here—for Socrates? For his audience? For the reader of this dialogue? We find, for instance, that his stand goes against the grain in that it disturbs and challenges prevailing social and moral arrangements; that his defense is radically *personal* in the sense that what hangs in the balance is his integrity as an individual, a teacher and citizen; that the defense is tightly reasoned and offered in support of passionately held but thoroughly examined beliefs; that it proceeds by taking up and apart the charges of the opposition; that Socrates' attitude is nonconciliatory even as he appeals to what is rational and good in the men about to judge him. All these features constitute the "voice" of this old man on trial for his life, the *ethos* of his *apologia* (in Greek: self-defense).

Suppose, we say, we extrapolate from this ancient philosophical discourse a sort of essayistic subgenre and call it "the apologetic essay." Do we actually meet such essays anywhere—*i.e.,* essays that construct such voices? What range of voices do we discern in them? Can the writing of such an essay answer to the motives of a college student in the latter days of the twentieth century? Turning to King's "Letter from Birmingham Jail," we find just such an apologetic essay, impassioned and brilliantly articulated, as though inspired by the same Socratic model, indeed honoring that model by explicit reference. The study of King's "Letter" concentrates on how its local stylistic effects and the amplification of the whole construct King's apologetic ethos, the "voice" defending the breach of unjust laws in the pursuit of justice. King's language is the sort of stimulus that impels quantum leaps in stylistic awareness and experimentation—when people start trying to write like King (as they almost inevitably do), they find themselves getting into sentences unlike any they have ever attempted. But the double encounter with Socrates and King is so awesome for many students that they begin to express vaguely sorrowful feelings about the state of their own uncertain, nebulous, shifting, half-articulated convictions. Partly in consolation —and to see how the impassioned apologetic essay may be attenuated in harmony with individual sensibility—we turn to Stevenson's "An Apology for Idlers," with its touches of clear-eyed self-assessment, its playful and distinctly ungrandiose, yet still deeply ethical, voice.

The task is this: write a fairly substantial essay (about 1,500 words) in which you defend or otherwise grapple with something of importance to you as a person, something that may go against the grain of prevailing values, attitudes, or practices—an action you undertook, a decision or choice you made, an attitude you hold, a value you espouse, a way of life you want to embark on. Make it something that, however marginal to others, reaches to the moral center of who *you* are and how you inhabit the world, such that without this thing you would not be the person you consider yourself to be.

While everyone is writing, and until the papers are ready, we begin each class by rehearsing aloud what various members of the class have in progress; the rest of each session goes into talking about one or another of the following recommended readings, all of which are in different ways informed by the apologetic spirit, however diffuse or submerged or softened:

Cornwallis, "Of Entertainment"
Thoreau, "Life Without Principle"
Du Bois, "On Being Black"
Forster, "What I Believe"
Hurston, "How It Feels to Be Colored Me"
Steiner, "A Kind of Survivor"
Theroux, "Cowardice"
Quammen, "Thinking about Earthworms"

One might add to this list one or more of the following student essays (see Part III of this manual):

Amy Wang, "Confessions of a Patriot"
David Levine, "Faltering Muse"
Eve Pearlman, "Having Things"

Skillful student essays are, in my experience, among the most productive teaching instruments in a course of this kind; they carry a conviction and a weight ("relevance," in the parlance of the 1960s) unmatched by published writing. The writer struggling with his or her own muddles is heartened by the proof that kindred others have managed to achieve clarity and a measure of beauty—that it *can* be done.

When the essays start coming in (usually by the end of the second week in this segment of the course), a few are read aloud to the class, normally one, at most two, per session, to give adequate time for critiques. To do this sort of intensive class scrutiny of an essay, a scrutiny as close and serious as any given to a published essay (see Part I of this manual), one needs a manuscript in hand to mull over and mark up; I make every effort, therefore, to supply xeroxed copies, in advance whenever possible, so as to give people time to prepare their critiques for the next meeting. Ensuing discussions lean heavily on the written *student* critiques provided for each essay presented to the class, the idea being that these represent the most concerted, hence the most authoritative, responses available. (My own critique is for the writer's own private use.) Revision of these apologetic essays continues as we move into the next segment of our course.

Irony and Satire (3 Weeks)

The apologetic essay, however modulated by uncertainties, ambivalences, or self-doubts, exacts and thrives on forthrightness: the "I" of such an essay must confront its issue head-on as an "I" staking out a place for itself without concealment or evasion. Irony, on the other hand, is the language of indirection; it does its work by *double-entendre,* subterfuge, and attitudinizing of various kinds—understatement, hyperbole, self-deprecation, pseudoanalysis, nagging, grouching, exploitation of clichés, skewing of the facts, and the like. For the essayist, irony presents opportunities for disguise and, as such, introduces dangerous pitfalls. It is the serpent in the garden of essayistic truth (see pages 703–705, *The Art of the Essay*); managed skillfully—*i.e.,* managed with a high degree of self-consciousness about what one's real motives are—it can be a wise serpent indeed, with a sting unlike any other.

In the classroom, ironic essays, especially in the service of satire (the indirect critique of evil and folly in whatever genre) make as great demands on the writer's verbal resources as they do on his or her powers of self-scrutiny. I sometimes begin this segment of the course with a discussion of ironic language, the ease with which it lapses into bad faith (intellectual and psychological escapism, moral laziness), and the relation of irony to satire. (Helpful in the latter regard are the brief and readily available treatments of these and related topics in M. H. Abrams, *A Glossary of Literary Terms,* or, more extensively, in *The Princeton Encyclopedia of Poetry and Poetics,* edited by Alex Preminger *et al.*) Or we may plunge right into the indisputable monarch of ironic essays, the greatest veiled polemic in English, Swift's "A Modest Proposal." The challenge here is to figure out, through hard and detailed analysis (see especially questions on irony under VOICE in Part I of this manual, p. 11) the answer to two basic questions: How do we know this discourse is to be read ironically—*i.e.,* that it works not as the "proposal" it purports to be but as satire? What are the targets of this satire—*i.e.,* what can Swift be after? Not to be overlooked or escaped in "A Modest Proposal" is, of course, the voice itself—on the face of it, the proposer's "I," so reasonable and humane, and yet. . . . He is both the key to Swift's irony and the linguistic embodiment of all that the satire aims at, *i.e.,* of its targets.

Through analysis, students become rapidly infected with wanting to write satires—at first because the moral/psychological inversions and the semantic tensions of Swift's discourse suggest a game of sorts, a device for fabricating a kind of anti-self. As they get more deeply into writing satires, however, students discover the snares of ironic posturing, the powers of satire to expose the essayist's sometimes inadvertent and muddleheaded complicity with the very things he or she most abhors. In fact, the meeting with this largely unsuspected and unacknowledged self is one of the great values of attempting satire; the ironic "I" becomes not so much a mask as a stripping away of deceptions and self-deceptions—that, at any rate, is how it works at its best. Sometimes there is mostly confusion, not unwelcome when it leads to discovering that one may be less sure of things than one had supposed (the opposite of what comes out in apologetic writing), that language may not be the transparent and unequivocal device one had assumed. Russell Baker's "The Flag" makes an excellent modern companion piece to "A Modest Proposal," portraying, as it does, a writer implicated in the very attitudes he pokes fun at.

Meanwhile, as in other parts of the course, I encourage additional readings with scheduled discussions to complicate our understanding of irony and to enlarge the possible range of ironic language and the voices they construct. Students who choose not to write full-fledged satires of the Swiftian kind may find inspiration in one of the following:

Fielding, "An Essay on Nothing"
Lamb, "The Convalescent"
Blackwood, "Portrait of a Beatnik"

The extravagant parody (Fielding), the sustained exercise in self-criticism by ironic aggrandizement (Lamb), and the slyly crafted social caricature (Blackwood) all make different demands on the writer's powers of observation and imagination and on his or her verbal resources and judgments. Irony functions more diffusely still, and more occasionally, in the following essays, where it emerges as a strain of the writer's sensibility, some characteristic way of experiencing and framing self and world:

Earle, "A Detractor"
Twain, "Corn-Pone Opinions"
Morris, "Fun City"
Atwood, "Happy Endings"

Jacques Whitecloud's "Guns" (see Part III of this manual) is a fine instance of an ironic voice serving both to assert a self and to question it. This piece is perhaps a contradiction in terms: an apologetic essay tinged with irony, or conversely, an ironic essay with a firm and insistently candid apologetic edge—the controlled articulation of ambivalence.

This segment of the course usually produces one longish essay (about 1,800 words) or two short ones; much rewriting goes on, much gradual gathering of insight into the workings of ironic discourses from the *writer's* rather than the *reader's* point of view. Even the English major who has written respectable critical papers about ironic texts finds that it is one thing to write *about* such a text, another to produce one from scratch. I sometimes reverse apologetic writing and ironic writing; the relative positioning of these two segments creates a very different course and a radically different experience for the student struggling to bring self and voice into some satisfying conjunction.

People and Places (5 Weeks)

Polemical writing, whether apologetic or ironic, renders the essayist's "I" problematic in ways that no practitioner can easily bypass or refute. How the "I" fashions itself in such discourses so as to be both cogent and truthful poses demands each writer must struggle mightily to satisfy, developing in the process a high degree of self-awareness, both rhetorical and personal. While the first paper in the course is clearly an exercise in reflection, the main focus on reflective writing comes at the end, during the last four to five weeks of the term. What I am calling "reflective" here is the "personal essay" conceived in the narrowest sense (not, of course, the working conception of *The Art of the Essay*): that blend of evocation, storytelling, and rumination that makes a piece come alive with all the humanity of the reflecting writer, the observing, sensing, feeling, responding, thinking instrument, so to speak, through which the essay's topic passes or is "reflected." The "I" of such essays feels powerfully "natural" to reader and writer alike; that is, reflective voices engage us perhaps precisely to the degree that they appear merely to be expressing some whole, stable, existing human identity apart from and behind the essay's language. In a successful reflective essay, the rhetorical "I" (voice) and the existential "I" (self) appear indistinguishable. The art of the reflective essay is thus the art of apparent artlessness, notoriously one of the hardest of all to master. For that very reason, reflective writing comes last in this course, only after the relationship of voice and self has been sufficiently disturbed to call into question both the naive notion of a "natural," or "real," voice and the pseudosophisticated notion of voice as a kind of mask, a "strategy" for winning over the reader. Even at that, there can be a lot of backsliding.

The experiential truth is, of course, that reflection is a productive activity, neither the transmission of preexisting "ideas," nor a rhetorical contest with the reader, but the groping after ideas by way of words, the reaching "back" into a largely unassimilated personal past or "out" into the world vibrating with largely inchoate meanings. A good reflective essay takes its writer on a journey, and, as we all know, who we are at journey's end is not who we were at the outset. The reflective essay cannot be the record of a mind—hence a self—made up; nor can it be a calculated pose. It must be the account of a mind in search of itself, "voice" generating in the work of writing some new "self" that understands something it did not grasp before, not necessarily an answer or insight or solution, perhaps only articulated complexity where before there was unexamined confusion.

We talk about these things not primarily in the abstract (though such talk has its occasional utility) but by looking at accomplished essays. To narrow the scope of options (we have only about five weeks left for some very hard and serious writing), we focus on reflective writing about people (the character piece or short memoir) and about places. Students may work up one longish (about 2,000–2,500 words) or two short essays during this final segment of the course. A certain intensity tends to set in at this point, for in addition to this new project everyone is still revising earlier work, much of which is, for the first time perhaps, starting to take on a really satisfying shape. (It will have become clear, at least, which essays might achieve completion and some degree of polish in the time left and which, though interesting, are probably beyond remedy for the time being.)

I often begin the readings for this section with old student essays. One of the most effective of these over the years has been Collin Harty's "Ray and I" (see Part III), testifying as it does to the fact that an account of another person, someone close to the writer, turns more or less explicitly into an account of a relationship, hence into a probe of oneself by indirection. It is the same discovery one makes in Doris Lessing's superbly crafted "My Father," the essay that appears to have been, in a distant way, a model both of Collin's piece and of Ki Jun Sung's "My Father" (Part III). Turning to student-written accounts of places, I have had good luck with Scott Witham's elegantly brief "Places"; Eben Klemm's "Home from Here" is from my most recent course, and its appeal to that group suggests this may become a stimulating model for the future.

Besides the Lessing selection from *The Art of the Essay,* other good readings about people, variously suggestive and instructive, are as follows:

Orwell, "Reflections on Gandhi"
Mitford, "A Bad Time"
Laurence, "The Very Best Intentions"
White, "A Slight Sound at Evening"
Walker, "Looking for Zora"

Laurence's piece is squarely an essay about an unusual kind of friendship. The other four are about people not directly known by the writers; yet, markedly, these essays convey an involvement, intellectual and emotional, that is ordinarily consigned to the "personal relationship." It seems to me that Woolf's "The Death of the Moth" can and should form a part of this group, for Woolf's tiny visitor rapidly takes on the features not only of all living individuals but of human lives in particular; if this ephemeral drama at the window is not an intense account of a relationship, I don't know what is. Two essays that treat the essayist's self almost as if it were another person, as if it were a "character" for reflection, are Johnson's *Rambler* #146, "In Pursuit of Fame," and Du Bois's "Guilt of the Cane."

As for good essays about places, public and private (sometimes, too, about the people in them), their abundance in *The Art of the Essay* needs no apology because a place—whether Addison's Westminster, Dickens's London, McPhee's Atlantic City, or Dillard's Galápagos—can and does set off just about every kind of thought capable of passing through the human mind, whether by way of memory, perception, or imagination. Here are some of them:

Earle, "Paul's Walk"
Addison, *Spectator* #26, "The Tombs at Westminster Abbey"
        Spectator #69, "The Exchange"
Dickens, "Night Walks"
Hawthorne, "Foot-steps on the Sea-shore"
Belloc, "The Mowing of a Field"
Leopold, "Marshland Elegy"
Lawrence, "Whistling of Birds"
Manchester, "Okinawa"
Morris, "Fun City"

McPhee, "In Search of Marvin Gardens"
Ozick, "A Drugstore in Winter"
Hoagland, "City Walking"
Momaday, "The Way to Rainy Mountain"
Rhodes, "The Death of the Everglades"
Rose, "Tools of Torture"
Dillard, "Life on the Rocks"
Naipaul, "City by the Sea"
Ehrlich, "The Smooth Skull of Winter"

The plentitude of readings for this final segment of the course encourages the sort of browsing that sets off memories, stimulates ideas, and generally frames the whole project of writing a reflective essay in a context rich with things to be tried out. Until the class papers actually start coming in (the third week usually), the class has more than enough to do, what with revisions of earlier essays to attend to and reports on readings people are finding valuable and interesting. My experience has been that these reflective essays tend to be the students' best work; earlier writing takes on the feel of an extended practice for these last efforts in which the elasticity of the essay form seems, finally, to be measuring up to the complexities of the writer's motive. Self situates and finds itself in voice: voice becomes the verbal habitat of who one feels one is, and, more radically, a way of knowing and being that person.

*   *   *

Materials relevant to Narrative A:

— The sections on Motive, Truth, Voice, and Praxis in "Essayists on Their Art," at the back of *The Art of the Essay.*
— Questions in section 2 of BEGINNINGS, p. 5; all of the questions on VOICE, pp. 8–11; and section 2 of CLOSURE, p. 12, in "Thinking About Essays," Part I of this manual.

NARRATIVE B

Necessity of a special kind mothered my invention of "The Art of the Essay," version B. One year I had the good fortune—and, as it turned out, the luxury—of having two sequential semesters of the course all to myself. I was to teach one section of it in the fall, another in the spring. Nothing prevents a student from taking the course both semesters because, ordinarily, there is a change of instructors, hence a new syllabus and a different orientation altogether. As the fall term gathered momentum, about half of my students (with an eye to preregistration) came inquiring about the spring course: What would it be like? Could they be in it? Meanwhile, new students were also coming around to find out about enrolling in "The Art of the Essay" the following term. Short of dismissing one set of applicants outright (the interested students from my fall section were among my best; the new ones looked promising), I clearly had to come up with a way of teaching "The Art of the Essay" the second time around so as to serve two very different and, on the face of it, incompatible constituencies. Spring semester had to be both a continuation and a self-contained, coherent new version of the course.

The design of course A, with its reliance on models (very loosely speaking), had proven to be demanding and commensurately productive. Term after term students rose to its rhetorical challenges and seemed gratified by the results. The notion of "voice" gave the course its focus and direction, while allowing freedom in the choice of what to write about. From time to time, I had sensed the pressure for an even wider freedom—to be allowed to write simply as one pleased—and I had been thinking on and off about how such urges might be accommodated in a course that would, like A, link reading essays with writing them—a course, in other words, that rooted the practice of the essay in its tradition as genre. The key to the new course lay in my observation (already noted) that the dynamic of writing essays and of sharing them with the class acquired special energy when the writer became so absorbed by some topic or problem that he or she would carry it over from one essay to the next—from an apologetic essay, perhaps, to an ironic one, or from there to a reflective piece. Putting this another way: students tended to get most excited about their work when they turned up, stumbled perhaps unexpectedly upon, a motive that exceeded the capacity of any single paper to explore and articulate it. One wanted to keep on writing, paper after paper, because one found there was more and more one wanted to know and say. Working from that observation, I determined that the organization of course B would place this feature of writing—the essayist's motive, broadly construed—at the center.

Two interesting problems suggested themselves: (1) how to create a class environment where freedom to choose subject *and* form would place demands on the writer equivalent to the demands of working from rhetorical models; (2) how to keep the essayistic pursuit of personal interests from losing itself in the very assumptions about self and voice that course A had been designed to challenge, with the result that student essays tended to grow at once more "truthful" and more truly sophisticated as essays. How, in short, to keep this new course from being a free-for-all (not a bad thing in itself, perhaps, but a distinct disadvantage if one is working in a tradition). I came up with two tentative answers, tentative in the sense that the course itself would test their utility: (1) given greater freedom to write whatever essays they wanted, students would be required to take on a proportionately greater burden of self-discipline as members of a writing community; (2) and as each member of the class struck out in his or her own direction of essay writing, the class as a whole would explore, practice, and learn to talk descriptively about style—how discourses work close up, at the level of words in sentences. Course A approached the essay by way of voice—the question of who is "there" in the words; course B would approach it by way of the linguistic forms through which voice articulates itself as prose discourse. Style is voice created by language: that was the link between the two courses. They were the flip sides of the same coin, different in appearance but cast of the same metal. Course B would thus be both an extension of A, so that it could work as a continuation if necessary and as a course on the essay's art in its own right.

To approach the essay so squarely by way of style meant encountering head-on the issue of just how well undergraduates can learn to write given their crowded institutional lives, how they can start to appropriate the wealth of verbal artistry that centuries of English prose have wrought. My key instrument was to be an old and old-fashioned one: imitation. I did not know (do not know to this day) how widely imitation is used nowadays in the teaching of reading and writing; my impression was that it might be viewed as slightly disrespectable among specialists in literacy, if not outright reactionary. I had little idea, moreover, whether students would enjoy reconstructing the styles of other writers, whether they could do so with any degree of skill or grace, or what difference it would make to their writing in the long run. I had noticed in course A how certain verbally ornate styles (*e.g.*, King's in "Letter from Birmingham Jail" and Norman Mailer's in a selection I sometimes used from *Miami and the Siege of Chicago*—the part about the slaughterhouses) tended to "infect" students without their seeming to be aware of it, to carry over into their own writing without apparent premeditation on anyone's part. They read these pieces, marvelled at their virtuosity, and when they came to write on their own, they wrote differently, not a little intrigued by what they had just done (or almost done) with a certain sentence or even a stretch of sentences. Something had disturbed the seemingly natural order of things that an individual "has" a style (somewhat like a nose, or a certain texture of hair—not, of course, a hair style), and that that is that. King "has" a style, Mailer "has" a style, I "have" a style. An individual, it now began to appear, could grow into a style, into several of them in fact, to discover in certain ways of fashioning words new—and possibly true—ways of being, of perceiving and feeling. Style began to look like a whole array of shoes, of every hue and texture, each of which fits quite remarkably well if one is willing to make the attempt at wearing it. Course B, rather than leaving stylistic enrichment and flexibility more or less to the accidents of influence, would deliberately stimulate experiments in style and guide each writer's stylistic development as an essayist by the device of regular exercises in imitation. These imitations would open up the stylistic realms of the possible; making those realms personal would be the task of each student essayist.

The luxury of teaching "The Art of the Essay" as a year long sequence stemmed mainly from the convergence in the second half of those two very different sets of students: the ones who were continuing and the ones who were getting started. From the first meeting it was obvious that I didn't have to work at establishing a writing community; I already had one. The people from the preceding term knew and respected one another as writers. They were easy with each other, and that ease set the tone of our interactions while their semester's experience with the essay calibrated the level of our interchanges about texts. The veterans already had a model of critical reading (see Part I of this manual) and thus a serviceable format for class discussion; the new people quickly caught on, and in no time, it seems, everyone was conversing with everyone else as though they had always been doing it in just this fashion. If any questions or puzzles turned up in one half of the class, the other half was there to elucidate. All I had to do was keep the whole thing moving.

I started out that semester as I have ever since in this version of the course, even when it is the only go-around for the year: with three weeks of intensive reading and discussion of essays, older and modern, while each member of the class works out a direction for his or her own writing during the term. On the first day of the fourth week, everyone has an essay written, to be read aloud; from that point on, the papers come in as prescheduled by individual writers. Reading aloud and critique of class essays alternate with separately scheduled exercises in imitation, while students are perusing essays in our book at their pleasure, as it were off-stage, writing up reading notes as directed for inclusion in the final portfolio, and leading class discussions on essays of their choice on designated days.

Here is a sample class schedule (based on a fourteen-week term) to show how these several activities might mesh from week to week:

Weeks 1–3
  Class discussion of assigned essays in text

Weeks 4–5
  Readings of class essay #1

Week 6
  Imitation #1; readings of new class essays

Week 7
  Readings of class essays; student-led discussion of outside reading (by prearrangement)

Week 8
Readings of class essays; imitation #2

Week 9
Readings of class essays

Week 10
Readings of class essays; imitation #3

Week 11
Student-led discussion of outside reading; readings of class essays

Week 12
Readings of class essays

Week 13
Imitation #4; readings of class essays

Week 14
Readings of class essays; student-led discussion of outside reading

When course B has to stand on its own, my only shot at teaching "The Art of the Essay" for a given academic year, the first three weeks become critical for consolidating the class, introducing students to the world of the essay and its tradition, and getting them started as self-reliant readers and writers expected to carry on their work largely behind the scene of the classroom itself. The focus of our first session is a passage read aloud from Woolf's "How Should One Read a Book?" It is the bit near the beginning of the essay, where she talks about asking of books not what we want them to give us but what they "can give us," of not dictating to an author but trying "to become him," of striving to be "his fellow-worker and accomplice" (*The Art of the Essay*, p. 222). I propose to the class that this is a way of reading they may never have tried or been encouraged to do. As students we are trained to be extractors of information and interpreters, not "fellow-workers" or "accomplices." (One may as well say it: collaborators.) To break the ice we may be allowed, from time to time, to free-associate with a text, give our opinion, and run on about ourselves rather than it. But we are not urged to inhabit the text as a living discourse, its paragraphs, sentences, turn of phrase, as if it were partly our own, its voice and style forever in the making before our very eyes and ears, as though *we* were somehow collaborating with the author in the work of essaying. We are not taught, I propose, to read like writers.

In "The Art of the Essay," everyone must learn to read in this new way. For everyone in the course *is* a writer and reads in order to become a better writer. Whether considering a published essay or one just created by a classmate, everyone must be concerned not so much with what it "means" or "says"—*i.e.,* the essay as argument in the broad sense—but with how the thing is *done*: how Bacon gets through his wonderfully economical single-paragraph account of what "studies" are for; how Addison meanders into a kind of beatific vision in that periodically built final paragraph, when all he has appeared to be doing is telling about an afternoon walk among the tombs because it seems an apt time of year to be talking about death. That a writer reads differently from other people, that he or she reads more sympathetically, more constructively, than the "critic" or the "student," is a fundamental premise of the course and a chief goad to self-discipline.

The first day's assignment is good for three weeks and has two components. One is this: try to read, day by day and like a writer, at least the following essays (which may vary from one term to the next, but the chronological spread is essential):

Bacon, "Of Studies"
Addison, "The Tombs at Westminster Abbey"
Johnson, "On Spring" or "In Pursuit of Fame"
Hazlitt, "On Going a Journey" or "On the Feeling of Immortality
    in Youth"
Lamb, "The Convalescent" or "Grace Before Meat"
Stevenson, "An Apology for Idlers"
Woolf, "The Death of the Moth"
Welty, "A Sweet Devouring"
Porter, "St. Augustine and the Bullfight"
Ozick, "The Riddle of the Ordinary" or "A Drugstore in Winter"
Steiner, "A Kind of Survivor"
Selzer, "A Worm from My Notebook"
McConkey, "In Search of Chekhov"
Dillard, "Life on the Rocks"
Rhodes, "The Death of the Everglades"
Walker, "Looking for Zora"
McClane, "Walls: A Journey to Auburn"

As they read these pieces, students are to ask themselves: What are these writers responding to in the world? In themselves? What interests and moves them as essayists? Everyone is encouraged to jot down any ideas—especially ideas for essays—set off by these readings and the ruminations they impel.

The second part of the first day's assignment is this: consider what you want to write about this semester. Make it something you care about, something you feel you could ponder and work at all semester without exhausting or explaining it away to yourself, something about which your feelings are sufficiently complex so that you can see yourself writing about it in deadly earnest, with biting irony, or lighthearted good humor, whichever you may come to feel like doing as the term progresses. By way of shorthand, we call this the semester's "topic." Everyone writes an essay on his or her topic for the class of the fourth week and prepares to read this essay aloud to the class. A topic may take whatever turns the writer pleases in the course of the semester; it may be stretched or modified in accordance with the writer's evolving interest in and understanding of the topic. This means, in practice, that individual writers are free to shape their essay portfolio entirely in accord with their own judgments.

Until the first papers come in, we discuss essays from the preceding list, starting perhaps with Bacon, Addison, Hazlitt, or Stevenson, and continuing with essays recommended by members of the class. At the conclusion of each session, we assign ourselves one (or at most two) such recommended readings for the next day's discussion. I lead these early discussions rather closely, working from chains of questions such as I detailed in Part I of this manual; as this exploratory critical model takes hold, we use it to the extent that it helps us to illuminate how successive essays work, focussing sometimes on only the most interesting and instructive aspects of craft. Our goal at this point is to learn from these writers how to write essays by looking at how they create theirs and by working through that creative process with them.

To keep reminding ourselves of what else is going on during these weeks of reading and discussion, we start off every session with a few minutes of informal talk about where people are in respect to the semester's topic and the first essays. I urge the class to try writing out, as succinctly and plainly as they can, what their topics are: a paragraph in which each person attempts to circumscribe the issue or problem or concern that will serve as the central topic of several essays. These paragraphs are circulated to me and one or two others for written responses (very likely, questions about what all the writer has in mind). By the final session of this three-week introductory period we all know pretty well what everyone is up to and await the first performance. During that last session, aware that the focus will be shifting to everyone's first essay, I give instructions about continuing the reading for the rest of the term. People are to browse and read in our book as they wish; everyone is to write from six to twelve notes on essays of their choice, concentrating on some aspect of craft that interested the reader *as* writer. (A reading note is defined as a unified comment, perhaps a single long paragraph, not exceeding 200 hundred words). People may turn in their reading notes for comments or save them all for inclusion in the final portfolio; everyone is encouraged to incorporate whatever they happen to be reading into whatever discussion is in progress in the classroom.

The writing of essays is at the center of all this activity, both for individual students and for the class as a collective enterprise. Over the years, students have come up with semester writing topics as varied as their own preoccupations, academic and professional orientations, and temperaments. In my most recent experience with this course (fall 1989), the topics tended to be on the whole more inward and concerned with questions of identity, as the essays by five members of this class, included in Part III of this manual, indicate. Shana ("Slick Styling") chose to write about the painful issue of mental illness as social and personal reality; Eben ("Home from Here"), very much taken by Didion's "On Going Home," wanted to explore for himself the ambiguities of home and of belonging; David ("Faltering Muse") was deeply interested in the multidimensional notion of "uncertainty" in the overlapping realms of his social, intellectual, aesthetic, and emotional life; Eve ("Having Things") settled, after several trials, on how possession and possessiveness work in her self-definition as a person and a woman; Jacques said he wanted to try to sort out for himself the question "What is good?" from the question "What is real?" These and other comparable topics turned out to be potent motives for writing and rewriting several essays whose boundaries were in some instances very sharply drawn by differences in focus, scope, and language and in other cases blurred or intersecting. Some students, that is, found themselves creating a group of distinct essays clustered loosely around a single problem; others considered themselves to be writing in essence the same essay from different angles and in different modes, working at it until they had achieved some measure of clarity and cogency answering to the impetus behind the writing.

As in course A, the reading aloud of these first essays is followed by brief comments from the class as well as substantial written critiques from me and one or two other readers. The reading aloud of these first essays takes us through the end of the fifth week, at which time everyone is already at work on a second essay (or a revision) while continuing to read published work. To organize the flow of papers from here on in, I ask each person to work up a schedule for turning in three to four additional essays (plus revisions) on the semester's topic; from these individually set deadlines, I make up a master schedule for the class of which everyone receives a copy. We now know exactly whose work is coming in when and thus what will be available for selection and discussion on a given day. The system of self-scheduling no doubt sounds more cumbersome than it turns out to be in practice. The degree of self-discipline and responsibility imposed by it is a distinct advantage for the operation and atmosphere of the class. Sufficient flexibility is built into the system so that if a given writer simply can't deliver on a promised date, prenotification and the stream of other essays flowing in almost certainly keep the process stable and dependable.

Starting in the fifth or sixth week, we alternate a day or two of short imitations with two, three, or more consecutive days of critiquing student essays. It is essential to sustain the momentum of these class readings and the writing behind them; at the same time, the occasional exercise in imitating a set stylistic model offers a break from the intensity of this process and eventually comes to be felt as an integral and productive part of it. In the past, I have drawn on the first three chapters of Richard Lanham's comprehensive and stimulating *Analyzing Prose* as the basis for these stylistic imitations and have concentrated on these aspects of style: the role of verbs in the sentence, the uses of grammatical connection, and what I call the "architecture" of sentences (see *The Art of the Essay*, pp. 725–730) according to principles of suspension and accretion. The Lanham chapters contain splendid illustrative passages from the work of famous literary figures (Woolf, Hemingway, Dickens) as well as from lesser known writers in various fields. These passages are surrounded by much good commentary, some of it exceptional in its analytic detail and its effort to link formal features of style with features of temperament, value, and outlook (what Lanham terms *motive*). The illustrations I have found most valuable as models for imitation are the short excerpt from "Time Passes,"—the middle section in Woolf's *To the Lighthouse*—illustrating Lanham's "verb style" (Chapter 1); the excerpts from Hemingway's *A Farewell to Arms* and from the opening chapter of Dickens's *Bleak House,* both of which Lanham presents under paratactic styles; and the excerpt from Lord Brougham's speech to the House of Lords in 1832 illustrating a hypotactic style (all in Chapter 2). (Although three of these passages happen to be excerpts from novels, the essay's versatility could easily accommodate any one of these bits of narration and description.) In connection with Lanham's Chapter 3, "Periodic Style and Running Style," I bring in literary models from other sources for one or two additional imitations designed to make students grapple with syntactic patterns of suspension and accretion.

In all, every student writes from four to five imitations (each about half a typewritten page, single-spaced) staggered over about an eight-week period. My instructions for these exercises are as follows: read and reread (preferably aloud) the illustrative passage many times until pieces or whole stretches of it start resonating through your memory; study it very, very closely, sentence by sentence, word by word; read and study Lanham's stylistic analysis of the passage, if he has one, and think about how it accords with your own construction of the model's style; now choose some suitable topic of your own and write about it in the style of your model, either imitating your model sentence by sentence or more freely, so as to structure into your prose the salient features of this style as distinguished by your analysis. (Sometimes the class as a whole may spend time analyzing a passage in preparation for the writing exercise to follow.) A caution to students: pick a subject that seems to you consonant with the style you are attempting to recreate; watch out for dissonances that might result in parody. (Parodic imitations, by the way, are always welcome and often forthcoming as extras, that is, on top of the assigned exercise. My experience is that parody, fun though it is, inspires only more parody; a style must be seriously felt to affect a student's habits and life as a writer.)

Students are asked to submit their imitations at least two hours before our class meeting, on a single sheet of paper, so that I can cut and paste all the imitations together end to end and run off enough copies for everyone. The reading aloud (and evaluation) of these imitations in class becomes one of the great treats of the course, for they tend to exhibit astonishing verbal and syntactic dexterity, more often than not under admirable control. Students surprise themselves and each other by what they have turned out. So great, in fact, is the astonishment of some that they may try to disown their imitations—"Well," they say, "I did this as an imitation, but I would never write this way in my *own* essays." Whereupon I (and perhaps others) point out that the imitation *is* the writer's "own" and proceed to ask why not: "Why *wouldn't* you write in some such way as this in an essay?" The fact that the answers are never very satisfactory can lead to a good bit of soul-searching, which, in turn, may set off experiment and transformations of the writer's work as a whole. Revisions of earlier essays may become occasions for a new kind of care with language. New essays may take on a subtly or markedly different verbal texture. An imitation may become the impetus to a whole essay; it may even find its way into an essay, suitably modified and integrated. What makes all these things happen to the extent that they do (and the extent varies greatly from student to student) is, I think, the simple fact that students enjoy the sheer challenge and the playfulness of recreating another writer's language; what starts out as a species of impersonation takes them into new terrain, both verbal and personal. The rich resources of English prose begin to offer new means for articulating themselves and their concerns as writers. Some students polish their imitations as assiduously as their essays, finding the process valuable for consolidating their development as analysts of style and venturers in the expressive realms of style.

The Lanham book has been for many of my students their first encounter with rigorous stylistic thinking; some of them continue with it on their own, well beyond what our class schedule permits. I occasionally hear from ex-students who still own the book (did *not* cash it in at the bookstore) and pour over it from time to time. Despite some terminological differences and taxonomic incongruities between Lanham's analyses and those presented in "Talking About Style" (*The Art of the Essay,* pp. 713–740), there is no reason the two approaches could not work in tandem, the material in my appendix on style being essentially an expansion of how I transpose what the class learns about style through imitating several of Lanham's illustrations to our reading and analysis of essays. Now that I have a book of essays with its own related discussion of style, the passages cited there and the larger contexts in which they occur might well serve as the basis for imitation exercises in future versions of my course.

I cannot emphasize enough that the study of style in a literary environment as richly illustrative as the essay, far from being an indulgence of the formalistically and technically inclined, is both fun and enlightening for quite ordinarily trained students interested in becoming better-than-average writers—in discovering that their "own" style may have a much greater range and a fuller resonance than they had supposed. In the practical context of writing and evaluating imitations, the study of style is an almost incalculably productive device for the student's development as a reader and writer. Imitations often occupy a place of honor in the final portfolio. This fact seems to suggest that something about these short prose trials of getting inside another writer's world has made of the whole semester's work a richer and stranger thing than one had imagined at the outset; that the student essayist in pursuit of the semester's "topic" has only begun to take his or her own measure, and that to begin is a very fine and exciting step indeed.

*   *   *

Materials relevant to Narrative B:

— The sections on Motive, Truth, Style, and Praxis under "Essayists on Their Art" and all of "Talking About Style" in *The Art of the Essay*.
— The questions in Part I of this manual, particularly those concerned with style.

PART III

Students as Essayists

Foreword

by David Levine

I was enrolled in English 388, "The Art of the Essay," during the fall semester of 1989. Five of the essays that follow were written at that time (Ederer, Klemm, Levine, Pearlman, Whitecloud); the other four were culled from previous classes (Harty, Sung, Wang, Witham). There was only one assignment for the entire term: to choose a theme and write a set of essays around that theme, exploring it from as many different angles as possible. This was, in short, an invitation to spend a whole semester working out, in prose, conflicts and issues and notions that had long been on our minds. For those of us who accepted the invitation an interesting thing happened: the essays grew longer and longer.

Our initial forays were timid affairs whose overall statements were as abbreviated as their length. This was due not only to the newness of the form but also, I suspect, to the nudity it imposes. The essay is the baldest of genres: the author cannot conceal himself behind the scholarly or the journalistic "we," is in most cases denied the camouflage of Factual Proof. He hasn't the anonymity afforded fiction's puppet master pulling his characters' strings unseen behind the curtain, nor can he take refuge in red herrings or long-lost uncles should his message fail to grip. Subtle as an essay's point may be, there is never any doubt as to who is making this point, as to who is assuming, with such arrogance, that others might benefit from these ruminations. There the author stands, stripped of all disguise, proclaiming, "This is what I have to say. This is how I feel. You would do well to listen." And if one doesn't have the conceit to say that, there's no point in writing an essay at all.

Most of us lacked this conceit, at least to begin with. Having been brought up to be modest, objective, and generally self-effacing on the page, none of us was egoist enough to risk droning on too long, to dig too deep. The result was that none of our first attempts was particularly interesting, let alone convincing. But through these half-starts we got a taste of what could be achieved in this medium, of its potential for sorting out, if not solving, the conflicts that so move and confuse us. The wall of humility eroded a bit, and we wrote. And then the wall crumbled completely and we wrote and wrote, and the more we discovered, I think, the more it seemed our discoveries were worthy of others' consideration, or at least of a written testament to the efforts we had made. But in either case the result was the same: an increased willingness to discuss ourselves and our observations on the workings of the world. Call it what you will, an increase in confidence or an increase in conceit, but without it we wouldn't have the work of the nine egoists who are about to have their say.

43

© 1991 Houghton Mifflin Company. All rights reserved.

Ray and I

by Collin Harty

Ray and I were good friends, but of an odd sort. He is an older man who has lived his life in the woods. I am a younger man, city-bred, who has dreams of cold deep rivers flowing north and the wild lands they intertwine. We see each other rarely and don't talk much when we are together. We used to always talk about fly fishing; we knew each other through the rivers. But today we don't talk much about these things.

Ray is a wonder with a fly rod. He has spend a lifetime perfecting his cast not just to catch fish but to know the rivers. He says that to understand the lives of fish you must first understand the lives of the insects they feed on, the cycles of the water they live in, the geology of the rock that retains it, the plant life at its margins, and on and on until the border between the fish's life and your own becomes fine. In Ray's mind there is no clear distinction between fly fishing and life, and the river encompasses them both.

He is a quietly heroic figure to me. Fly fishing is the discipline through which he has shaped his life. I find it a graceful discipline and a very noble life. Ray is what a part of me would like to become, so seven years ago I picked up a fly rod, as I would a tool, to begin trying to carve the quality of his character into mine.

Fly fishing was my obsession for many years. My classroom was the headwaters of the St. Joe River in northern Idaho, where I spent five summers working for the U.S. Forest Service. The St. Joe River is located at the end of sixty miles of one-lane dirt road. Few people travel it unless they have some obsession of their own. At its end there is only the river and you.

My first casts were clumsy and ill-directed, but through sheer determination I learned quickly. I spent almost every evening of those summers walking the river, turning over stones to learn what lived beneath them, observing what ate what else, watching how the water moved over the rocks and how its course changed as the summer progressed, and practicing my casts so they would roll out straight and drop with the softness of a hair on the water. I became sensitive to subtle changes in this living system from one month to the next, then from week to week, and even day to day. The river became a friend.

During those days Ray was two thousand miles to the east, but he was with me in spirit every evening on the river. Every action, every decision I made was based on what I thought Ray would do. He was my mentor through the power of imagination alone. In the off-season I would visit with him and we would talk of fly fishing; he was the teacher and I the student. I would show him the flies that I had tied,

44

© 1991 Houghton Mifflin Company. All rights reserved.

and he would inspect them. He was quick to criticize and slow to praise. "Tie the wings on your Light Cahills more vertically," he would demand. If he was silent I knew I was doing fine; silence was his expression of pride.

Even when we were together I needed imagination to learn his lessons. There were always hidden meanings. "Fish the biggest, most dangerous holes alone," he often insisted; then he would hesitate, to make sure I sensed his grander meaning. When I nodded in understanding I made sure to look him straight in the eye as confirmation. We talked of fly fishing but were trying to say much more. We were two men from different times and different backgrounds who needed a way to communicate—fly fishing was our language. The fish were the nouns; their strike, the verbs; a tight cast, a beautiful rod, and the evening light the adjectives and adverbs; the river, the topic sentence. Messages were passed in subtle ways. There was much reading between the lines.

We gave each other a great deal this way. He was an example to me of the grace of a disciplined life, an example of the sense of wonder and respect that can come to a person through something as simple as eight feet of graphite and six weight line. In his eyes, I think I was his hope for the future, an extension and refinement of what he felt was important in the world, a promise to life beyond his own. Two years ago, however, we arrived at an impasse our language could not overcome. In my last summer on the St. Joe I decided to give up fishing. We have been at a loss for words ever since.

The day I quit fishing was nearly perfect. It was typical of the rhythmic pattern I had developed with the river. At dusk I had walked alone down to a big hole I knew well, just above a beaver lodge where the water was deep and calm. I knew the Caddis Flies were beginning a hatch, and the fish knew it too. I waded out hip-deep. I knew to place my fly on the far side of the river, just below the riffles at the top of the hole, where it would land gently, drift along a low granite cliff, and be swept into the calm water at the end of the wall. If my rhythm was correct, it would be then, right then, that a cutthroat trout would rise and strike. It might not be a keeper, but I knew I would get a strike; by now I felt the river held few secrets from me. And that is just how it happened. Everything was as planned, just as I had learned it should be, just as I pictured Ray would have done it—that is, until I held the fish in my hand.

I did not know that I was going to quit when I went out that evening. I still don't know exactly what peculiar arrangement of conditions led me to my decision, but I do remember that fish. It had fought hard, but my four pound test was tougher. It was alive but limp in my hands and no longer fighting—just waiting. For its part the battle was over. In the brief seconds that I stood staring at what I held, a new sensation rose in my mind. I awkwardly describe it as the thought of the fish. It was a very alien sensation, one that felt ill at ease passing through a

© 1991 Houghton Mifflin Company. All rights reserved.

human mind. I looked into its cold Osteichthian eyes and saw the fire for life. It felt through its scaly body the sheer tenacity of a life beyond my own, and as the river tugged at my legs, I recognized that it matched an equal drive within myself. There was indeed a fine line between the fish's life and my own, and the river encompassed them both.

The trout did not expect to feel the rush of life in his veins again. I lowered him into the water and moved him gently back and forth so the water would pass through his gills. When his blood was rich with oxygen I released him. The river simply rolled on past. For my part I had come too close to the fish and had been allowed to see too far into the world of the river to ever want to risk hooking a fish again. The river could as well surrender me. It was not fear I felt, but awe.

When I tried to tell Ray why I quite fishing, I failed. There were no words in our language to deny the necessity of its own existence. Ray simply said, with a distant look, "Oh, you mean you were never really a fisherman," but I'm not sure if he was truly listening. Talk of fishing had distracted him. I could see in his eyes that his mind was elsewhere. He was intent on the motion of a trout circling with uncertainty around a manmade fly somewhere in his imagination. He was anticipating the strike and then the fight. He was feeling the calculated arch that is put into a fine rod by the tug of a trout. He was moving toward a point where his mind was more caught up in the thoughts of fish than in the thoughts of men. Ray does not fish for sport; he fishes because in a small way it allows him to transcend divisions in life, divisions between land and water, youth and old age, scales and flesh. He fishes because it nurtures within him compassion, respect, and a sense of the beauty of life.

Ray and I find the same beauty in rivers. That beauty led me to quit fishing; it makes Ray fish more passionately. Neither is right; neither is wrong. Seven years ago I may have simply picked up the wrong tool for the task at hand. It was Ray that I wanted to know as much as the rivers. In an attempt to do so I may have relied too heavily on a language I could not master. As our language faltered, so has our friendship. But we don't talk much about these things anymore. Now life is not as vivid without his quiet wisdom or as inviting without the hope we gave one another for the future. I am not sure now how our future will go. It is the thought of the fish that I find most encouraging—its sheer tenacity and unwillingness to give up. It passes vicariously through my mind, stirs my imagination, and flows out through my pen onto paper. I have picked up a new tool now, and have written this for you, Ray. It is through rivers that we can know one another again.

© 1991 Houghton Mifflin Company. All rights reserved.

Slick Styling

by Shana Ederer

I was having my hair cut the other day, and, as I sat down, the hair-dresser, a woman named Pat in her early fifties, tapped my shoulder in a friendly way and asked about my family—how is everyone doing? Is everyone healthy?

I never know when people ask me how I'm doing if they're asking because they really want to know or because they're the sort of people who pride themselves on being attentive to others. Sometimes I smile and say, "Fine, thanks. How about you?" Sometimes I answer, but not really the question asked: I might tell them what I've been doing instead of how I'm doing. Most of my answers fool most of the people, most of the time.

A few of my friends know just about every little wink and flinch and grimace my face is capable of producing, and when they ask how I'm doing, there's no sense in trying to duck smoothly underneath the question and emerge on the other side, untouched. Sometimes I assume, just for convenience, that if you don't know me well enough to see those little winces and flickered smiles, it's because you don't want to know what they mean—don't want to know what I mean when I answer a question like "How's it going?" So I fix myself carefully in friendly conversation, and I say the sorts of things that could be said between any two people, anytime and anywhere, because then I don't have to sort people out; I don't have to decide how much of me they really want to see. Sometimes I can catch funny little hooks in a voice, hooks which snag and grab and hold fast the meat of my existence, but sometimes voices are as slippery and textureless as people, and Pat's was one of those.

Pat fell into my murky middle ground; she wasn't completely un-known, she was a family friend, of sorts—a long time ago she was friends with my mother and father, and maybe, if I had inherited some of their Pat-friendly blood, she was my friend too. But I didn't know how strong the connection had been, much less how eroded and corroded it might have become. I looked at the slick plastic wrap I was wearing and decided it would probably shed real conversation as easily as cut hair; a hair salon is no place for answers. It's no place to open your mouth and unleash words like you snap off a dog's leash, letting them jump and run and howl—it's a place to smile, to answer without answering, to ask questions without questioning.

I knew better than to track muddy paw prints all over a flowered linoleum floor. I wasn't going to answer, but then I started to open my mouth and the "Everyone's fine, really" just hung there, in the back of

47

© 1991 Houghton Mifflin Company. All rights reserved.

my throat. It didn't want to come out. It stayed there, firmly lodged underneath my right tonsil, and I found myself taking a hard swallow instead. I couldn't figure it out. In all the times I had said "Fine, thanks," this had certainly never happened before. I was stuck. I had no choice but to give a real answer now, even though I was sitting in a red plastic swivel chair and my hair was slicked back wet, waiting to be cut—my ears stick out when my hair is wet. I could imagine all those heads turning on me at once, plastered with hair crimped and cramped and curled and pressed, ears swiveling and hovering and honing in on me, on the disruptive conversational wave I'd surely let loose.

I've always thought that some places are worthy of real conversation and some aren't, and hair salons are on the first list. Or I thought they were. It seems silly when I think about it, but I always thought the walls would cave in if you said something like "My grandfather just died" in the deli section of the supermarket, in between ordering salami and a half pound of potato salad. I don't know what I thought were right places to talk about something like that, though. I never seemed to think it through very carefully, figure out just when I was permitted to abjure "Fine, thanks" and talk with whatever words happened to spill out. Sitting on a riverbank watching the sun set, cast glowing orange and pink against the sky? Walking under stars made sharp, cuttingly brilliant, by the low light of the waning moon?

The problem is that most of us don't spend our days by the river watching the sun go down under pink clouds, or our nights walking under the stars. I haven't sat on a riverbank in months, and when I walk late at night I'm often alone, and tired, and if I look around at all it's to make sure that the man walking behind me stays a good safe distance back there. I track from red brick to cement block, and I walk over dead grass and strewn garbage outside and shag rug and newspapers inside, and everything seems to work its way inside me and coagulate, forming a cork or a plug. When I find myself stuck in a place like that, a building or a room which seems so unfit for the weight of human habitation and speech, I have a hard time preventing the grey walls from creeping into my speech and flattening it, so I don't really speak very often at all.

Not that I don't talk. I'm pretty good at making noise, and maybe that's why I was surprised when my "Everything's fine, thanks" refused to come out and make its polite appearance, keep things fluid and moving so they couldn't be pinned down. I thought about it when those words got jammed up inside, and I decided maybe they just didn't like the company. I mentioned earlier I wasn't sure which answer to give Pat, and that's because I have sort of a list for people, too. Some people are worthy of real conversation and some are not, and I wasn't sure where to place Pat on my list.

© 1991 Houghton Mifflin Company. All rights reserved.

I lived in the same house for eighteen years, and I hate to admit it, but most of the people on my real conversation list are people I grew up with, people I met before kindergarten and before fear of people, and long before I began making these silly lists in my head. I've since lost the recipe for instantaneous trust, and sometimes it's hard to weave new ties without it. How can I demand someone's attention if my words aren't really words, if they're just part of a set of noises which seem to be universal to the human condition?

I think maybe that's why I found myself sitting in that plastic chair with those words stuck in my craw—I'd been chewing them over for too long, and they didn't taste good anymore; they didn't feel good rolling off my tongue. They'd been there too often. In the past year or so I've often found myself talking despite my lists, despite the picky little voice which tells me not to bother and never seems to catch a sore throat or get hoarse, like I do. I decided not to worry if my "Everything's fine" was having a problem, if it thought that the surroundings or the audience wasn't up to par, even for its meager performance. I answered people and they listened, even if they didn't fit into my tricky time-and-place equation.

I lived then in a little rat box whose greatest virtue, beyond sheltering me wonderfully from Ithaca weather, or Ithacation, was being just like all the other little rat boxes around it, no matter how we disguised it with posters and wall hangings. I had never cried in front of anyone since I came to college. But when I broke down in front of my apartmentmates last year, they sat down next to me and listened and handed me kleenex, even though the carpet was one of those indestructible indoor-outdoor marvels and the whole apartment was grey and ugly and assaultively sturdy, with cold white walls and right angles all over everywhere. Right angles are hard and square and not made for people who are round and often think in circles or electrified wiggly lines, messy people like me, trying to trust and confide. All those angles were meant for people who don't reflect themselves off of others; all those clean lines told me that I should keep everything in order, emotions included.

But I sat there and cried, and at some point I realized I was living there, spending my days and sleeping my nights in its cold modern shelter, and maybe I didn't have to wait for the right time, the right people, the right place because, after all, how right can anything be? My roomies weren't perfect, but they certainly weren't any worse than I was. I started wondering why I was waiting for the right place—what if I never got there? It had made sense to me before. No, not in the grocery store —it's crowded and loud, and how can you be serious when you're pushing a wire bucket on wheels? Not in the green and yellow seat of the Chevette, where the engine revs and clonks and you have to shout to think, and not at McDonald's, where people are busy masticating their

© 1991 Houghton Mifflin Company. All rights reserved.

food before it gets cold and the french fries turn to little sticks of grease, and certainly not in class, where everyone seems like they're asleep or bored or fascinated with taking notes in ordered little outlines, making subtopics and indentations and tiny Roman numerals—how can anything so sloppy, so unpolished and disordered and unconsidered, make its way through all that without collapsing on itself?

When I came to college I discovered a set of corollaries: never talk during a co-op meal at a large dining hall over stuffed shells; never talk in the minute or so you have to kill before class, there's no point in beginning what can't be finished; never talk in the morning, everyone is crabby and late; never talk to someone with an exam or a paper or project due, they may hear but they won't listen; and never talk at parties. Parties are meant for noise, not talk, and I'm not complaining about it—there are times when noise is all I can handle, when I need the loudness to drown out everything else. Every once in a while, with lots of alcohol, I find myself talking to someone at a party, sitting in the cold quiet outside and saying absolutely everything that comes to mind, so I guess that's not entirely true. But then I usually don't remember much of what was said; it's an evaporating honesty, and I wake up as groggy and uncommunicative as I ever was.

All of this stuff was hanging in a tenuous balance as I sat there and thought about what I should say, what I could say, to Pat. She tapped me on the back to remind me to sit up straight, and her scissors started snip, snip, snipping away. I don't get haircuts very often and I've never been a big fan of hair salons; I always feel like I don't know how to carry on the right kind of conversation. Maybe I didn't mention this before, but I don't really like nodding my head and smiling at people, even though it's almost a reflex reaction, and I don't like talking about the last exam I took, the sweater I just bought, or how much work I have to do. Things like that lubricate conversation—it's like greasing up a lock with lead so the parts move easily, instead of fixing it—but at some point in time they build up and jam the works. A lot of the time I open my mouth and that's what jumps out, and maybe it's because I spend too much emotional or intellectual energy chasing things like that around, I don't know. But I wonder sometimes if I talk like that because everyone around me thinks like that, never letting themselves off the leash of everyday thought and emotion. I can never decide—is it me, or is it them?

I thought last January it was them; it was everyone else who was so ground into what they owned and did and wanted to own that they couldn't talk about what they were. Where they were, who they were. After being subjected to so many conversations about Porsches from Grandma at graduation, and so many happy hours with people standing in little circles swirling their beer in plastic cups before they spoke, and so many whispered discussions in the library Sunday afternoons about

© 1991 Houghton Mifflin Company. All rights reserved.

last night's party and who was there and what they did, I was sure I was right. I just shouldn't talk to some people, except to nod my head and smile and tell them how my classes were going or what I did last night, and that was that.

I watched Pat pull my hair into sections and pin it up with pink and yellow plastic clips in the mirror. There was certainly no need to carry on a real conversation here, in a hair salon, where people didn't even stay honest with their superficial selves, where they were dyed and poked and trimmed and filed into other, more streamlined forms, the way polite conversation is shaped at a gathering of distant relatives. I had no right to be honest here. But then could I really be honest anywhere if honesty was merely a function of time and place, a guise I assumed when the moment was right, the stars were aligned correctly in the heavens above and I held my listener's attention in my fist?

I looked at Pat in the mirror and something came loose inside me—I think it was the filter I use to strain things from what I'm saying. When I opened up my mouth again the "Everything's fine" had dissolved completely—it wasn't blocking up my throat anymore, I could breathe and things were clear.

"My brother's been hospitalized the past few months with schizophrenia, so things haven't been all that smooth lately," I said. There it was, sitting in midair, something I never thought I'd be able to say in a casual conversation, something I usually swept over and around and under but never aired out in speech. I never knew what would happen if I just came out and said things to people—my mother told me I was even a quiet baby—so I didn't. I imagined the conversation would fall into silence and the listener would glance away, never really looking back at me until the conversation moved to other, easier things. Or maybe I didn't imagine it. I can remember stumbling into that silence, and maybe that's when I began my list, when I began scrutinizing listeners and talkers and rating them, sometimes before they had spoken themselves.

Pat's scissors kept on clipping away, snipping off the ends which were deadened and frayed, and I couldn't hear anything but sliding metal moving through hair. She didn't look up. But she tousled my hair as she began to speak, sailing across the line I had breached to meet me on the other side, ruining all my lists and all my understandings of places and people I had thought I couldn't talk to because they wouldn't know how to listen. "My son was schizophrenic, too, although that was a long time ago now."

I felt like I had snuck into somewhere I didn't belong as we began to talk: I was walking across posted land, ignoring the glare of the orange and black signs and their forceful, forbidding clarity. Part of me wasn't ready for what she had to say because there is a security in rules of the sort I had, in not knowing too much about anyone or letting them

© 1991 Houghton Mifflin Company. All rights reserved.

know too much about you. And it's hard to sit and listen, really listen, when everything you've learned tells you that this is not the time or the place, when the sun is shining bright outside with a sacrilegious cheer and everything around you is plastic and fake and maybe, just maybe, the people are fake as well.

I always thought that people related as much as they were able, that they spoke as much or as little as they could, given what they had been taught, lessons learned that I had never seen. But I never turned the equation around to see that I was a little short. I never suspected that many of the people I had relegated to my superficial list were there because, like Pat, they were waiting for me to cross the line, for me to venture outside of the polite constructs we use to shield ourselves, before they disarmed themselves of their conversations about bars and beer, about work and cars. Maybe not all of them. But some, to be sure.

It was my turn to fall spinning and silent, quiet in a peculiar gratefulness, when she asked if my brother was just schizophrenic. We were moving fast and far from beauty-salon banter, from everything safe, away from the people who didn't know that my brother was, after all, "just schizophrenic." I'm grateful that my brother is schizophrenic because he could be dragging around even heavier labels, like Pat's son.

My brother could be schizophrenic and manic-depressive.

Pat's son was sometimes violent, sometimes abusive, and he ended his downward slides at the police station. No treatment was effective. Or almost no treatment. There is always a last resort, and for bipolar depression, it is electroconvulsive shock therapy.

"We'd have to take him to St. Mary's every few months, and they would shock him a little—ECT is what they call it now, I guess. It really saved him. He'd go back to college, finish his classes, everything. He even graduated from Michigan State."

I think I had noticed with her first sentence that everything was in the past tense, that her son *was* schizophrenic, but I didn't want to think about it too carefully, I didn't want to know why. When schizophrenia is woven into the mood swings of major depression, the web is almost never broken; I knew that. And I didn't think I wanted to know any more. I didn't want to swallow the broken glass ends of her son's story. I didn't like the power her few words had over me. I still felt the barriers, still felt the harsh glare of the linoleum floor and the light conversation all around us as if it were an assault, and I waited, listening, because there was nothing else I could do.

She swiveled me around sideways in the chair and picked up a black plastic comb. "The best, the kindest thing about it, was that he couldn't remember things, he couldn't remember the things he'd done when he'd gotten bad, and rowdy, like . . ." Captive to my imagination, I could see Eric with all his blond hair shaved off, scalp bare and bristly with electrodes; I could hear phone calls in the middle of the night from the

© 1991 Houghton Mifflin Company. All rights reserved.

police. I could image what those voices on the phone might have to tell me, things that would stand in my memory like vacated buildings, making me grateful for the wrecking power of electroconvulsive shock therapy, the fresh blankness it might bring, if not to me, then to my brother. And I knew why I kept lists.

I nodded and listened as hair was swept from beneath my feet, and Pat scrutinized my bangs to see if she'd trimmed them to the same length. A television played a videotape from the World Hairstylist's Championship, an event, Pat informed me, every bit as prestigious as the Olympics—if you cut hair for a living. Pat reached for a can of hair spray—I almost never use hair spray, but it makes hair stylists so happy that I always let them—and she said, "You know, he ended up killing himself."

The words hung out there in the air for a moment, and they spun around, and they settled. The woman in the next cubicle had gone slack-jawed. Her mouth was hanging open like the mouth of a fish—was she breathing through her mouth because she didn't want to smell the pungent chemicals from her perm, or speechless because a woman had finally won the World Hairstyling Championship, beating all those big-name guys, or was she gawking, gawking because she'd eavesdropped her way into a little more than she'd bargained for? Pat was still running her fingers through my hair, checking length, and I could hardly move. I had bungled my way into one of those quiet spaces most of us guard so fiercely, and now I didn't know what to do with myself—I was afraid of stumbling and tearing things, of tripping and ripping holes in whatever scarred tissue was still vulnerable to injury. Afraid of saying something wrong, I said nothing which could be wrong, I slouched in my chair and let her talk.

She set down the hair spray with a clink, on the counter. "They quit giving shock therapy—there was some political thing about it . . . He just got worse and worse, and they wouldn't treat him, and he took his own life." She reached for the blow dryer and plugged it in, asking, "Do you usually blow dry your hair? What I'd like to do, you probably don't use mousse, but I'd like to use a little mousse. . . . You'll see, it'll look great."

I nodded or murmured something in assent, and I closed my eyes as the hot air hit my face and scalp. The light was too bright and I wanted to take off the slick plastic coverall I wore, shake the cut ends of hair off my shoulders. Pat turned my hair back with a little round brush under the stream of warmth, and the conversation died away in the blow dryer's comfortable noise. In a minute or two she would swing me around to face myself again, and I would look in the mirror for a moment. Then I would get up and walk to the front desk, past the lady with the fish mouth and over the linoleum floor, shaking myself clean.

© 1991 Houghton Mifflin Company. All rights reserved.

Maybe I would say good-bye, or maybe Pat and I would just nod at each other as she smiled and waved her next customer into the chair.

After I'd paid I turned around and found myself staring into the face of Marie Hoban, a friend I hadn't seen since high school graduation. We had played soccer together—I was left wing and she was my back-up at half, although sometimes she played sweeper. I smiled and she smiled back, and she offered me a bit of pizza—I don't know why she had pizza in a hair salon—and I said, "Just fine, everything's just fine," almost before she opened her mouth.

© 1991 Houghton Mifflin Company. All rights reserved.

My Father

by Ki Jun Sung

Listening to 1500 All News WTOP, my father drives, understanding only half of what is broadcast. This has been his English class for his thirteen years in the United States. In the passenger seat, I lean against the window and door, sit on my hands to keep them warm, and catch up on the sleep I have missed this winter break.

The motion of the car stopping and the sound of the ignition being turned off awaken me. Trying to shake off the sleep and the cold, I trudge across the parking lot and follow my father into one of the entrances of Y. B. Auto Body and Engine Repairs.

Inside the garage, a perimeter of cars forms a second set of walls within the permanent gray walls. It is dark and cold because the necessary amount of lighting and heating for such a huge space would cost too much. The chill is exacerbated by the usually open garage entrances through which much of the heat escapes and by the high ceilings which steal whatever remains. The dust from yesterday's sanding is everywhere —on the cars, on the floor, in the air. And soon more will settle on the clothes, hair, and skin, and in the throats and lungs, of the workers as the workday begins. The workers here do not wear dust masks because the moisture from their breaths, trapped in the masks, invites frost. They just blow their noses at the end of the day.

Smoking his first cigarette of the day, my father speaks with a couple of his co-workers who are Korean, like him. In fact, most of the workers at Y. B. are Korean (Y. B. stands for Yong Bae, the owner of the shop). They speak of the weather, the traffic, the elections and riots in Korea. I unlock the tool cabinet and set up the tools we will be needing for our current job. Some mornings I speak to Bob, the son of the owner, about the Redskins or the Orioles game. Today Bob is not around, so I turn on the heating lamp that is used to dry the plaster on cars and stand in front of it, hands in pockets, knowing that I should not be doing this since I will only be colder later.

Eventually work begins and it will not end until nine hours later with a half hour of lunch in between. Squinting, with his second cigarette dangling from his lips, my father squats, crouches, and examines the dented quarterpanel of a yellow Subaru with his hands. Touch reveals the nature of the damage better than sight and dictates where and in what order to start the repair. Standing, I watch, ready to take any orders. Inevitably, my father will ask me to fetch a tool which I neglected to bring out earlier or which is needed for a difficult angle of approach. I fight off the coldness by trying to ignore it and wonder if he is cold. He does not complain or show the symptoms of a person wishing

55

© 1991 Houghton Mifflin Company. All rights reserved.

for warmth. He never shivers, stamps his feet, rubs his arms, or blows into his hands—habits I have tried to conquer since they seem only to make me feel colder. He proceeds to disengage the quarterpanel of the car—there is interior damage, the extent of which he must determine. Encountering a stubborn nut, too large for the air wrench, he speaks to me for the first time today and asks me in his only proficient language to bring something.

"A what?" I ask in my native but foreign tongue. He realizes that I do not know the Korean term for the tool he needs. But neither does he know the English equivalent. He describes it to me: a wrench. A wrench with a variable mouth and a screwing adjuster. Something about adjusting it with your thumb . . .

"A monkey wrench," I offer.

"A monkey wrench," he asserts in Korean. I confirm to myself that I am not familiar with the word. I retrieve the tool from the cabinet, and in a rare moment of expressed curiosity, my father asks me to say it again in English.

"Monkey wrench." I pronounce it slowly.

"Mung-kee len-chee." He repeats. By tomorrow, we will both have forgotten how to say monkey wrench in the other language.

I do not really know my father. We hardly ever engage in conversation unless my mother is with us. And even then, it is only an indirect conversation. If we say anything at all, it is directed to her. My mother is, if not verbose, a very verbal woman, always asking questions and telling us about the meanings of her dreams the night before. My father and I usually just listen, answer a "yes" or "no," or, sometimes, mildly scorn my mother for her superstitious nature.

My father is a silent man. Therefore, I find him an almost inscrutable and a somewhat unapproachable figure. I do not inquire about his inner or past life. Does this mean I am not curious about him? I sometimes wonder what his response would be if I asked him to tell me about himself. What was it like to grow up on a farm in Inchon? How did it feel to grow up without a mother? What was it like to be sixteen and a private in the navy during the Korean War? Does he wish to return to Korea some day? Then I wonder if I will ever ask him such questions. Probably not; old habits are tough to break, and sometimes there are reasons why the habits developed in the first place.

I am very small, maybe four or five years old. Our family is returning from an outing, a visit to a grave site. It is a summer afternoon; I am wearing shorts. I ask my dad to race me to the end of the footpath. He laughs and then agrees. Nervous and excited, I concentrate all my potential energy and field of vision on the designated finish line and nervously wait for the signal to start. My father counts down: "Hanna, dul, set . . . go!" I run. I feel almost like Superman, I am going so fast.

© 1991 Houghton Mifflin Company. All rights reserved.

Tears are forming in my eyes from the resisting air. I am halfway there. But where is my dad? I cannot hear him behind me. I turn my head and look for him. He is there, almost exactly where we began. He looks as if he is running but is making hardly any forward progress. Can he be that slow? Can I be this fast? An innocent pebble, a rebelling root, a hiding hole, I am not sure which, but I trip on it and fall and cut myself above my right eye. I am crying and I hear hurried footsteps approaching. My dad picks me up and wipes my head with a handkerchief. He tells me that I am all right, but I continue crying. He sets me on his shoulders, holds my arms out, and runs toward the end of the footpath. As we cross the finish line he yells, "Ki Jun Sung—the winner!" But I did not win. I fell. My dad carried me here.

I am ten or eleven years old. I have developed an interest in sports— friends' influence. My father never plays, watches, or discusses this tradition of male bonding. In our backyard I am throwing a football up in the air and catching it and dropping it. My father has finished mowing the lawn and (on a whim?) asks for the ball. I toss it to him not knowing what to expect. In a clapping motion he catches it. He looks ridiculous: his legs are straight, his rear end is sticking out, his head is twisted away from the ball, he is wearing brown polyester socks in orange K-Mart rubber sandals. He heaves the ball back to me, and although it comes to me it is all wrong. He pushes instead of throwing, and the ball travels perversely, rolling end over end, instead of in a spiral. I throw it back to him and we continue this briefly until dinnertime.

I remember these events because they are two of the very few memories that live in the space of my mind reserved for the times shared by father and son. There were no weekend fishing trips or man-to-man talks. There were no lectures, reprimands, or advice. There was no encouragement to join the basketball and the baseball teams and the Cub Scouts of which I became a member. There was no praise when I brought home straight A's in the third grade, two years after I had encountered the English language.

My father used to be an angry man. Although the anger has diminished over the years, I remember nights when I would hide in my room while he shouted at my mother in the living room. I did not hear what he was shouting about. Perhaps I chose not to hear. I remember waiting and praying for silence and wondering why he was sometimes so angry. And there were nights when he would return home very drunk. I would be awakened by his retching and cursing in the bathroom while my mother would gently speak and whisper to him. And some nights I would be awakened by his fits of yelling as he slept and dreamt. He would wake up, walk around the house in the dark, settle down in a chair, and smoke. Today he no longer drinks or shouts, but he still has those dreams. Sometimes when I am up late at night I can hear him

© 1991 Houghton Mifflin Company. All rights reserved.

cursing somebody in the darkness of his dreams. But he no longer awakens from these dreams.

I wonder if he was always angry. Perhaps anger was all he had when he grew up as one of five sons without a mother; when he was chosen out of the five to be drafted during the war since everyone else eligible for the draft was needed on the farm and only one male member per family had to enlist; when he, as a farm boy, encountered malice from others in the navy; when he had to go to school for the first time in his life after the war so that he could find employment; when he had to adjust to the impersonal city life in Seoul; when he had to make a living for his family in America as a 7-Eleven cashier.

There is one memento of my father's past in our house. In black and white, he stands lean, tall, and handsome in front of a resplendent garden. Wearing a narrowly lapelled jacket, a thin dark tie, and slimly tapered pants, he holds a cigarette between the index and middle fingers of his right hand. The features of his face are readily accessible from this picture; they are not buried within the flesh, wrinkles, and darkness of middle age. They are not typically Korean: a high rectangular forehead, curly hair, a bumped nose, full, dark, round lips, a wide mouth, deep-set eyes, a significant cleft in his chin, subtle cheeks, and thick eyebrows, the El Marko eyebrows that cap the features that some would say belong to an Italian or Spanish man. Italian, Spanish, or Korean, he is a handsome man. Physically, he must have been admired by many women. Did he enjoy the company of many women? He and my mother married although she did not want to. The marriage was her mother's wish, the highest command in Korea.

My father works without rest, tirelessly. A delicate balance of strength and finesse is the *satori* of the auto body mechanic. Slamming the sledgehammer to straighten the frame beam requires all the muscles of the body to concentrate on the target and work together to produce the fluid and apparently effortless swing that will carry the impact of a wrecking ball and the aim of a sniper's bullet. A couple of strong hits to unbend, a couple of slight taps to straighten.

Even the simple task of removing a screw requires mastery. It seems easy enough—turn the screwdriver to the left to unscrew, to the right to screw. But a row of screws used to take me three times as long to remove as they did my father. There is a skill involved; your grip and your forearm must form an extension of the screw, a straight line. The point between the screw and the screwdriver must be locked by your weight. The turning motion must not break the line. Grip, press, and twist simultaneously. Release your grip and untwist. Repeat. A difficult screw used to make me look inept. The screwdriver would slip and lose contact with the screw, my elbow would fly out of alignment, and a couple of difficult screws later I would be rewarded with blisters on my palm and fingers.

© 1991 Houghton Mifflin Company. All rights reserved.

The day passes slowly. It is better not to look at the clock. Your stomach will tell you when it is time for lunch and the diminishing light will tell you it is time to go home. The day consists of pounding, hammering, screwing, unscrewing, tapping, flattening, bending, straightening, pulling, aligning, fitting, welding, cutting, sawing, drilling, sanding, plastering, priming, blasting, smoothening.

I work beside my father, slowly learning the job he had to learn when he quit as a cashier at 7–Eleven. This job is more suited to his temperament; it is direct, there are no formalities of greeting, it is manual labor. I will work at this job for as long as I have vacations to come home from school. My father will work until he can no longer pick up a sledgehammer. I look forward to other jobs beyond this one, beyond college. This is my father's last job. After it is done, he will wait for the end of this life.

Five cars are renewed and the day is done. We wash our hands and my father changes into the uniform he will be wearing tomorrow. Listening to Power 105 WAVA, I drive home bobbing my head to the music. If the day has been unproductive, the weather and the traffic especially bad, my father will utter his only axiom for driving: "Don't follow that car so closely!" Today he sits back and stares ahead at the road, with a crack in his window to smoke his last cigarette of the day.

© 1991 Houghton Mifflin Company. All rights reserved.

Confessions of a Patriot

by Amy Wang

Yes, I am a patriot, strange as that may seem to some who know me well. They know how I sneer at President George Bush, how I gag at the mere thought of his vice-president, J. Danforth Quayle. They know how I bemoan a country that has the money and resources to send space probes beyond Jupiter, yet can't figure out what to do with the two million lost souls who call the streets home. They know how I fume at a nation that elects people like Orrin Hatch and Jesse Helms to the Senate and pays attention to Tipper Gore when she organizes a movement to censor rock lyrics. Tipper. What *is* her real name, anyway?

But I love America. The obvious analogy is a man who kicks his dog constantly but won't let anyone else do the same. Sometimes I can't stand this place, but I know I'll never leave. It's my home, and I have sunk my roots in deep. Perhaps too deep, but as the child of immigrants I really had no choice. Imagine yourself floating in the middle of the ocean, no land visible anywhere. If you saw a raft, wouldn't you grasp it, hang on with a grip that turned your knuckles white? Well, my parents' departure from their homeland is the ocean; America is the raft. And my knuckles are white.

The first time I had any consciousness of America as a nation was in the summer of 1976—the year of the Bicentennial, fittingly enough. I was six going on seven, and I lived in Pittsburgh. To me, Pittsburgh *was* America. I had seen maps of the United States and I knew of other cities like New York and Chicago and Los Angeles and Toronto, but all of them were unreal, shadowy places. All except Toronto, which I visited every year—but that was in Canada, so it didn't count.

Then in school we had a bicentennial party, and everyone was asked to wear red, white and blue. I just happened to have a dress which was all those colors, but I had outgrown it. I went to school in a red shirt which I hated, and sulked in a corner watching everyone else having a good time. It didn't matter that they weren't exactly draped in flags either; I felt I had somehow failed my country by not putting on the most patriotic outfit possible. Ten years later, as a bored young suburban middle-class self-styled liberal, I would cynically proclaim the Fourth of July "a crock." But in 1976 national spirit was strong and I felt like an outcast.

I did get to see Pittsburgh's bicentennial fireworks, however. And I remember seeing on television the elaborate celebrations in New York City, with the Statue of Liberty. As the hoopla began to die down I left the country with my mother for an eight-week visit to Taiwan. My father had left two weeks before. It was my mother's first return to the

60

© 1991 Houghton Mifflin Company. All rights reserved.

country she had left in 1967 as a newlywed. As the plane circled over the Taipei airport before landing, she began crying. I was too busy watching the lights on the runways to notice.

It was there, in Taiwan, that I realized America was a nation. To my relatives, I was "the American." My cousins were always pestering me to say something in English, and their parents smiled indulgently when I couldn't remember the Chinese equivalent of what I was trying to say. My grandmother was a little shocked at how freely I ran around and shouted and got dirty. She thought little girls should sit quietly at home reading or helping in the kitchen. Well, I did sit quietly and read—the adults were all fascinated when several of them got into a vociferous discussion one day and I never noticed, although I was just five feet away. I had a book with me and was oblivious to what was going on around me. But when I finished the book I tore down the stairs and ran screaming down the sidewalk with my cousin and his friends, nearly bowling over several startled pedestrians. Only boys did that in Taiwan, and not many of them.

When we went out strangers always stopped and asked if I was an American. My relatives would grin proudly: "Yes!" For a while I wondered how they knew; I didn't think I looked any different from my cousins. Maybe my clothes? I studied the way my girl cousins dressed but couldn't see any difference. Then my mother told me it was the way I walked. I stared at her, even more puzzled. What did she mean? I walked like anyone else; there was nothing wrong with the way I walked. Maybe she meant the way I talked. I knew I had an accent. But was it that obvious?

She explained to me that I carried myself differently from the other children. Because I lived in a country where children were free to run around on the streets, a country where adults winked at childish mischief, I moved with a confidence and self-assurance that Taiwanese children lacked. In America children often dominated dinner table conversation and were allowed to give opinions which were listened to and respected. And in American I had independence; I could make the decisions that would affect my life, decisions on education and career and marriage. I was unencumbered by centuries of tradition that decreed me a slave to my elders whims. So I viewed the world as my oyster and acted accordingly.

I was starting to get the idea that being an American was something special, maybe even something to be proud of. But it didn't really hit me until one day, in the middle of lunch, when I heard my uncle calling me. We were eating on the second floor of his house; the first floor had been converted into a general store. I ran downstairs and found my uncle standing out front with a tall white man. "Amy," said my uncle to the white man and gestured at me. The white man looked at me quizzically. "He's an American. He wants to buy cigarettes," my uncle explained in Chinese. I immediately got behind the cigarette and candy counter and

© 1991 Houghton Mifflin Company. All rights reserved.

clambered up on the stool. "He says you want to buy some cigarettes," I informed the man.

For a moment he looked as though he'd been shot. "You speak English?"

"She American," interrupted my uncle.

The man looked at me in amazement. "How old are you?"

"Six," I said. "I've lived in America all my life. I'm just visiting. He's my uncle. I'm from Pittsburgh. I was born there."

"Pittsburgh," said the man thoughtfully. He chose his brand and paid for it. Holding out his change, I asked, "Do you want some matches?" as my uncle had taught me.

"Yes, please," said the man. He still looked slightly dazed. "Do you go to school?"

For a moment I thought he must be stupid. Then in one of those rare flashes of insight, I saw myself through his eyes: a small Chinese girl with a tomboyish haircut who looked like a dozen other small Chinese girls with tomboyish haircuts, perched on a stool in a musty store in the middle of Taipei, chattering about Pittsburgh in perfect English.

"I'll be in third grade next year," I told him.

"That's nice," he said automatically. He stood looking at me and my uncle, clutching his cigarettes absent-mindedly. "Well," he said. "Goodbye."

"G'bye," I said, hopping down from my stool. I stood by my uncle and waited for the man to leave so I could finish my lunch. He nodded to my uncle. "Goodbye," said my uncle, nodding rapidly and smiling toothily.

As the man walked away, I ran back upstairs to the table. But when they asked me what had happened, I turned suddenly shy, squirming under their questions. They had to wait for my uncle's return to find out what had happened. When he told his story, they all found it quite amusing. But I only grinned, red-faced. How could I explain that in the two minutes, maybe five, of the encounter, I had suddenly and startlingly discovered that I was an American? An invisible bond stretched between the tall stranger and myself, and all because we were both citizens of the political entity known as the United States of America. After that episode, whenever I was introduced to someone, I always informed them that I was from America.

I returned to America that fall, and I have not been back to Taiwan since. I am not sure whether I want to go back or not; I think I am a little afraid of finding out how truly Americanized I have become, how wide a gap now stretches between me and my relatives. In the fourteen years that have passed since my trip, I have only become more aware of my feelings for this country. I can make all the usual arguments. Freedom of the press and speech and religion. Government of, for and by the people. Natural beauty. Cultural diversity. National wealth and a high

© 1991 Houghton Mifflin Company. All rights reserved.

standard of living. Educational and occupational options galore. The individual gets first priority. The American Dream—rags to riches. The American Promise—anyone can make it. All this, and more.

My parents forsook everything they knew so their children could grow up here. It was not a lightly made choice. They had just gotten married, they were financially dependent on my grandfather, they spoke only a little English, they knew no one here. But they came, lured by the Dream and the Promise. The Chinese phrase for America is "mei kuo." It translates as "beautiful country."

I feel I owe a debt to this country for what it has done for me. I can't pretend it has been easy growing up here. And my mother reminds me that as the child of Taiwanese—and hence Chinese—citizens, I have dual citizenship and thus dual allegiance. But when I fill out forms and come to the question that asks, "Are you a U.S. citizen?" I always unhesitatingly mark "yes." I never think of this country as The States; that's what my Canadian cousins, foreigners, call it. To me, it's America. When people tell me to "go back where I came from," I just smile. Hey, I have no problem with that, racist and snide as it is. I came from here. America is my country, mine, all mine, and they can't take it away from me; after all, it's the only one I've got. I knew that the day the tall American walked into my uncle's store and asked for a pack of cigarettes. Hey, I'll even go along when the good ole boys in D.C. finally plunge us into hell everlasting. Never mind the brimstone and sulfur: the flag's fireproof now.

God bless America—dammit.

© 1991 Houghton Mifflin Company. All rights reserved.

Places

by Scott Witham

In general, I am a dissatisfied man. In terms of habitation I mean. Always moving. Vagrant. Incessantly searching for a room with a view, a seat by the fire, a nest in the trees, a fortress in the wilds. A place, in short, to call home. But only for a while. My attention wanders, and I am off, bearing my longing, and my memories, with me.

What qualities do places have, to bring forth such inconstancy? What powers to loose and bind my faithless interest? Or perhaps more accurately, what sovereignty do I give these places to claim my attentions? Writers are especially prone to this act of empowering, for it is in the nature of their craft to attend to the places they inhabit, to personify the physical landscape through their work. They describe the places they have been as if this were important, as if this attending could inspire something by way of revelation. Perhaps this is what attracts me to writing. Places, and my memory of them, are central to my imagination.

Gertrude Stein said of her home in America, "There was no there there." She was at the heart of the matter, naming the intangible way places move us with their distinct personalities, or lack of them. We all see places differently, but we all see them, and they affect us. Some are foreign and forbidding, others welcoming or poignant, some both familiar and terrifying. Even if we feel nothing for a place, we acknowledge its power through our indifference. We have reacted.

The names of cities have always stirred my imagination—Rome, Marrakesh, Budapest, Los Angeles—each distinct and vibrant. There are other places, less famous, which perhaps move us more: the tree in the field, the house across the street, the corner of the kitchen. We all have these places, our private storehouses of memory. I am attached to mine, and it gives me a great delight of ownership. I do not suppose I am alone in this. As we collect places in our memory, image after image, each connected with an emotion, we begin to see the story of ourselves in a sort of skeletal form. We compare these images, as if sorting through an intimate attic of past lives. Each new place we encounter depends on the last for its meaning, each new comparison bearing the burden of all those that went before. In the end, places are empowered by what we bring to them.

This is agreeable to me. I am nostalgic by nature, and I do not begrudge the power places have over my imagination. It is the search for new places that is disconcerting, as if my memory can not exist if held still and must move forward to remain fresh. I crave new places simply to facilitate the remembering of old ones.

64

© 1991 Houghton Mifflin Company. All rights reserved.

Gertrude Stein went to Paris, along with many other writers, to realize a "there" there. But they did not escape their memories. They wrote about them. James Joyce went to Paris, too, but only to write about the Dublin he left behind and never saw again. He found the essence of one place while living in another.

This is a striking fact, which speaks to my own restlessness. I can, in a sense, see only behind me. When a place is left, when an experience is over, only then can I gather its meaning. When I am in Europe, I write about America, and vice versa, for my memories seem to crystallize simply by leaving the places of their origin. When I was living in Sri Lanka, I was besieged by images of the past, as if the very foreignness of the place reawakened all that was familiar to my imagination. Sometimes this awkward trait is so strong that the present does not seem fully real until it is a remembered past—in other words, until it is a story, one more episode to add to my personal mythology. I can remember being in a place thinking, "I will remember this," almost removing myself from the experience, looking to some future point when I could review all that happened at my leisure, somewhere else.

When I was in my rooms at Oxford, I relived scenes of childhood: the smell of a horse in the Midwest, a snowy evening in New York, the back garden in full bloom. In a small village on the Indian Ocean I was again in those college rooms; in the Quad outside the window, in a student pub off the High. Do I hear the sound of that small village, the slap of the waves and the giggling of children, more clearly now than I heard them then? It almost seems that I do. And I see myself on that beach, my long hair and my white clothes, as if in an internal mirror polished by distance and time. Even now, the ice on Cascadilla Creek, the huge oaks on the Arts Quad, a party in town and a face in the library, all are material for some future recollection. And I feel that old restlessness, mingled with curiosity, wishing to hold my life still and look back, to see what I am like.

© 1991 Houghton Mifflin Company. All rights reserved.

Home From Here

by Eben Klemm

> Over the hill between the town below
> And the forsaken upland hermitage
> That held as much as he should ever know
> On earth again of home
> —Edward Arlington Robinson

I have found that the night can be magic, a perfect synthesis of lighting, calm, sound and fury, but only under particular circumstances. Around nine or ten o'clock, after the suitably lurid vestiges of the sunset wash away the sweat of a summer day, a massive wind rises out of nowhere, typically a precursor to a storm. But no storm comes. Instead, the wind carries an unexpected dose of warm cleansing air, surrounding, surprising, sanctifying. The night feels like spring and sounds like fall, as the gusts churn through the regiments of maple leaves. The silhouettes of trees writhe in tandem. If clouds dominate the dark sky, their deep blue shapes contort and mutate and drive rapidly eastward. If not, all the stars in the universe stretch a silver chain mail across the darkness, above the susurrus of the nocturnal fauna: the peepers, the crickets, the owls. A flash, and a tinge of heat lightning rumbles through the somber hills flecked with the fleeting golden dots of fireflies aglow in the cool black grass.

This kind of night—I could fill the Library of Congress with words that attempt to describe it and still never quite get it—happens haphazardly. For me, it occurs only at home in Sharon Springs, and very rarely. Last summer, it blessed me twice. Once, during a college friend's visit, we sprawled, holding down the highest hill on my farm and, acid-emboldened, felt the wind and clouds suck down the night. The other time, a night of stars, I sat on my roof, the breeze blowing through me as if I were a skeleton, and wrote to another college friend. On nights like these, I feel perfectly happy, and perfectly content where I am.

Usually, the imperfection of Sharon Springs—its dullness, ignorance, decrepitude—plague my mind and mask my content. I spend a lot of time noticing and recollecting the drawbacks of this place where I grew up, proving to myself how bad it is. But why should Sharon Springs be a perfect place? I confront my hometown, take it apart, house by house, tree by tree, person by person, ask it, "What have you done to make me what I am?" Do I approach it like an alien descending in a spaceship, inspecting it from above as a globe transforms into a state map, into a local road map, and the clouds pull away and houses appear, until I can see the peeling paint, as Sharon Springs separates into its parts? Or

© 1991 Houghton Mifflin Company. All rights reserved.

do I start with me in the center and reach out in concentric circles to the town as a whole?

I haven't the faintest idea by whom or when or why Sharon Springs was founded, nor do I care. I wasn't born there; nor will I die there. Trying to sleep at night, I stare at the corners and walls of my room which appear naked because I've left my posters at school, and I count the nights that remain in this room. I describe the town's milieu to city kids as "bumblefuck." I missed Sharon Springs Central School's homecoming weekend this year and last—and I feel moderately pleased about that. But I have no memories of living anywhere else.

Sharon Springs lies approximately fifty miles west of Albany on Interstate 20, the Great Western Turnpike. This road was the aorta that once sustained dozens of small towns across the state. Dewey's thruway, which runs just ten miles north of Sharon, betrayed them, left them to wither in the oblivion of dead neon motels. The highway dips down a steep hill into the village, pauses briefly at its only stoplight, and climbs back out again. Whether it is the downward slope that naturally speeds cars up, or the insignificant mien the town presents to 20, travelers tend not to stop. Until the late seventies, AAA listed Sharon Springs as one of the four worst speed traps in the continental United States. The local cop, Babe, had a deal with the town justice to ticket anybody who lacked a local license plate. Immortality: last semester, a Cornell professor who'd been there recommended to his class that they never speed through Sharon Springs ("It's OK," I said, "Babe's dead."). Someone made an incredibly lowbrow film in Sharon, *I Drink Your Blood,* and for sound effects Babe got to fire his gun, the only time he ever did.

Two pathetic billboards, sagging into themselves, guard the town from Route 20 on its eastern and western approaches:

SHARON SPRINGS
HEALTH SPA OF CENTRAL NEW YORK

This summer, the Chamber of Commerce sponsored a new slogan contest for the signs. My family planned to enter the contest, but then we found out that the prize was dinner for two at the Park View. Losing is better than dinner there, the only restaurant ever that lacks a corkscrew.

A little way past the western billboard lurks an insubstantial dirt road, in taunting contrast to the four-lane asphalt affair which engenders it. The road, officially named Hazzard Road, creeps past maple trees, cornfields, and meadows for half a mile until it terminates alongside a hugh two-story Victorian badly in need of paint and two new porches. Cobwebs stock indelibly to the windows and green goose shit stains the back porch. A friend from Schenectady, visiting for the first time this summer, told me, "You have a beautiful house." She saw the vintage gingerbread trim, the commanding view of our pond, two parents that were happily married. I never thought I had a beautiful house.

© 1991 Houghton Mifflin Company. All rights reserved.

I've lived there sixteen years, and I know every flaw in that house—the unrenovated west wing, the hidden side with the fifties tarpaper faux brick siding, the waterstains on the arches my father installed in the living room ceiling. What house are you looking at?

Still, when I envision my house of the future, I don't do much but fill an empty space in my mind with details from this one. There exists in my mind no definition of home other than that of the old Parsons mansion just outside Sharon Springs. But this definition lacks a certain completeness, doesn't fit perfectly like a favorite pair of bluejeans, so I shove it to the rear of my cranium and take circular rides on long metaphysical trains of thought, asking myself, "What is home?" The places we call home are but different rooms in the house of our lives. We make our way from room to room, on an eternal search for the most comfortable chair. I've attempted to slam the door to one room behind me, but my right foot caught itself on the threshold. I struggle, I curse and I heap abuse on the room that binds me, but I haven't freed myself yet. Close the door completely, and I sever a part of myself. I go adrift in time, trapped like a top-hatted gentleman in an antique postcard, the ink browned by age.

You should see a picture of my parents in 1972. His hair is almost as long as hers, and her hair goes way past her shoulders. Very Haight-Ashbury. They fled San Francisco when the sixties died and crime moved in, just as they had from New York City five years before that. They found one hundred sixty-five verdant acres stretched into hayfields, thick woods and a three-acre lake. On the first day they visited, a brilliant red fox darted from underneath the porch of the gutted house and vanished into the thicket. The house, about a century old, and the land, carved as the last glaciers left it, originally made up the estate of Seth Parsons, the local hops baron. The remnants of an official croquet course are still visible. Hops smut, Prohibition and the Depression killed the Schoharie Country hops business; the land passed into the hands of the Hazzard family, dairy farmers before that lifestyle became a daily trial and a social sin. One day, Jim Hazzard senior let a little too much sun get to him: he ignited the hay in his cow barn and, amid the screams of roasting bovine, shot his family and himself. "You know what done it to him?" Old deaf Mr. Larkin, a glint of malicious pleasure in his squinty eyes, told me, "Wimmen."

No local would live there after that, so the Sharon Hunt Club purchased it to have their beer parties. They partied; the house fell apart. Then my parents discovered it, and dooming their progeny to a humdrum rural existence, borrowed $28,000 from friends and renamed the place Red Fox Farm. A photograph of them in front of the house on the day they moved in looks more like an ad for hurricane insurance than an icon of happy homeownership. The house is on the verge of collapse; the repair work ahead of them is reflected in their eyes. But they were happy, for at last a barrier lay between them and the urban

© 1991 Houghton Mifflin Company. All rights reserved.

decay they sought to escape. If I resent having grown up in a dull, rural environment, my parents bear an equal distaste for their upbringing in the exact opposite medium.

For two years we had no bathroom.

Route 20 cuts through Sharon so that passers-through completely miss its essence. The highway tells you that the local ice cream place is not a Dairy Queen and that the convenience store is not an A-Plus. It bears the name BJ's Pretty Good Groceries, and having once moved across the street and changed owners thrice, nobody knows if a BJ ever owned it. The current proprietor chain-smokes menthol Kools and dispenses political theory in agreement with the politics of whomever he happens to converse with. Only once have I seen him skip a beat, when some walking jetsam asked him for coffee and would he mind please telling him what month it was. Across the street from BJ's, on the other side of that solitary stoplight, squats Sharon Motors, home to Ralph, the bluest tongue in town, and Ralphie, Jr., who dwarfs his dad by about two hundred pounds. The sight of him bending over makes strong men weep. He lives in a trailer with his equally hefty girlfriend and their new baby. The garage is languishing; Ralph is dyslexic, and Ralphie dropped out of school, so neither one of them can decipher new and imported car repair manuals. Frustration: "These people, they come to me wit these new imported cars they can't drive, an say they got problems, you know, I feel like goin up to them, and takin a leak in their front pocket, sayin, all right, now you got problems."

Turn north at the stoplight, as if you were searching for the thruway, down the dugway past the buildings that used to house the local Zen center, and you discover a different Sharon Springs. Downtown, summer town. "Jew town," as many natives call it. The sight of buildings of warped wood and ancient paint assails you, aided by a flank attack on your nose from the smothering stench of sulfur, like month-old eggs. Crabgrass bursts through the sidewalks, cracked like Pompeiian mosaics. The facades of former hotels offer hints of past grandeur from beneath the trappings of wild grape vines. Welcome to the springs of Sharon, and to its past.

In the summer, the locals shrink to a minority, replaced by hoards of solemn, black-robed men and kvetchy women in wigs and flowered dresses. They traipse all over town, oblivious to everything—the locals, the smell, the through traffic—but themselves. The only traffic jams in Sharon Springs build up waiting for a petulant Hasidic Jew to cross the street. Their disdain for us ignorant goyim is matched by our own redneck suspicion of them, and both we and they spend our summers in fearful dismay of our forced coexistence. Each June several hundred members of this sect, strangely mystical in comparison with our own selves, appear here, and disappear again after eight weeks, to reappear next June in slightly diminished numbers.

© 1991 Houghton Mifflin Company. All rights reserved.

They are the last in a lineage: the Pavilion Hotel, the Vanderbilts, the Roseboro Hotel, Theodore Roosevelt, the Magnesia Gazebo, Martin Van Buren, Columbia Hotel, Imperial Baths, Ulysses S. Grant, Oscar Wilde, the "Baden-Baden of America." A hundred years ago, Sharon Springs stood on an equal footing with Newport, Saratoga, and Bar Harbor. Summer nights featured classical music concerts under ornate gazebos, to balance the summers days' medically approved therapy of sulfur gas inhalation and mineral water for bathing and drinking. The wonderfully pompous architecture of the late Victorian era dotted the hillsides as summer homes for wealthy urbanites. A railroad connected Sharon Springs to the rest of the world.

Time, as it does with alarming ease, passed. A misty daguerreotype made a century and a half ago tells more about the town than a Polaroid taken today. Sharon crumbled, bursting like a noxious bubble of sulfur dioxide. Hotels fell, burning or sinking slowly like great cruise ships, testaments to vandals, summer homes only to furtive makeouts and adolescent beer parties. Snowmobilers and dirtbikers make sure the railway embankment doesn't go to waste. The complete annihilation of Sharon Springs as a resort town is stayed momentarily by the presence of a dying generation of devout Jews, in search of a minor substitute for the classic mineral baths they once enjoyed in prewar Europe. Employees at the boarding houses and the last hotel speak of serial numbers on arms and of lonely deaths in hotel beds. Meanwhile, the town, assuming the eternal presence of the wandering Jew, proceeds to downgrade itself. This summer, I sneaked inside the Roseboro Hotel, where Theodore Roosevelt stayed. The four-story edifice leaks and shudders and sags terrifically towards the center. Rain and raccoons and local thugs have done their part. I took some hotel stationery from the main desk, colored cream with age. A low, wooshing sound permeates the building. An investigation in the cellar revealed a broken water main gushing torrents into the foundation. The town and the village government both know about it; they're waiting for the other to deal with it.

Every time I look downtown, only the ugly catches my glance before I toss my head and look away. I wonder if I search for reasons to elevate and separate myself from Sharon Springs. Perhaps I believe that if I refute my town's existence, the way it insinuates itself into my character and experience, I avoid the small town hick label I affix to my own back. Do I assume the boondocks heritage, or am I looking for a defenseless subject to blame my inadequacies upon? Maybe I just foist my own ignorance and shortcomings upon the warped town that fostered me.

Of course, if the town seemed warped to us, my family must have seemed equally bizarre to them. When we first moved to Sharon Springs, we were the type that made people say, "There goes the neighborhood." Our hair was too long, we associated with those Zen people, we swam naked in the lake. Worse yet, we didn't seem to belong to any church,

© 1991 Houghton Mifflin Company. All rights reserved.

and my parents didn't send me to school—the fact that I was three years old was beside the point. Early in our tenure here, my father asked a woman on a snowmobile to leave our property, unknowingly arousing the ire of Sharon's most fork-tongued gossip. My father later found out that he, naked and brandishing a gun, had chased her off the farm. And that he and my mother planned to turn the farm into a camp for black juvenile delinquents and drug dealers from New York City. A petition asking the Klemms to please leave Sharon circulated the town. But familiarity grows like weeds, and the town ran out of reasons to fear us. My mother has been on the schoolboard and my father trades crudities with Ralph. If there is a social structure here, my parents have broken into it.

Some things, though, never quite die. My brother learned how to drive last summer. The day after he first drove down Route 20, we found out that Noah Klemm had been seen drunk-driving, *during rush hour*. My brother may not yet be experienced enough to drive a perfect straight line, but here there is no rush hour!

"This school is firmly stuck in the fifties, and we like it that way."
—School Superintendent, 1975

"Smaller is better."
—School Superintendent, 1988

Sharon Springs Central School graduates a senior class of less than thirty. This limits class character, meaning the school's numbers of amazingly memorable and utterly forgettable people are unfortunately small. I graduated along with two soldiers, one girl pregnant and another already a mother. And people said I was ready for whatever the world had to offer me. But for the first time last year I drank from what I thought was a real fountain of knowledge, and reflecting on what high school had given me, found SSCS a dry gully. I spent last summer all but hiding from my former classmates. They are mnemonics for a time I do not remember with pleasure. Conformity ruled that small school with an iron hand; my memories of those hallowed halls are stonewashed and hair-sprayed. I spend too much time now wishing I had done this or said that back in high school—I hate to think that my main thought about secondary education is that I should have done it differently. As jaded about my past as anybody, I rise above it by kicking it back into ancient history, to forget, and to keep it there by encrusting it with memories I despise. I corresponded with only one classmate last year; in May, because he lacked the guts to buy them himself, I mailed him two condoms so he could lose his virginity.

The games I played when I was a kid—I possessed one hundred sixty-five acres of a fantasy kingdom to mold in whatever image I pleased. As a child I recognized the boundary between myth and reality; I just didn't

© 1991 Houghton Mifflin Company. All rights reserved.

care about it. An eight-year-old can walk forever in the tall grasses of summer and successfully escape attention, save for the rustling of the tips of timothy and crab. The discovery of British redcoat fungus bedecked in morning dew, or a shy walking stick camouflaged by the precise green of the plant it's on, provides a thrill equal to any discoverer's joy. If the wood darkens maliciously for adults, who see a home to danger and suspicion, to a child it glows with green and gold, each leaf a facet in a living emerald, interpreting the rays of sunlight according to its own whim. We build shelters and forts with boulders and rotten branches and battle each other for the sanctity we believe they contain. Older, I lead a girl I've just met deep into the woods to show her a cave I once found. We make love instead. This incident, of course, ruined the woods for me. I no longer remember myself doing battle with imaginary trolls beneath the glittering veil of foliage and recall instead the first confusing and bittersweet initiation into the pleasures of the adult flesh. I can't use such a place to represent just one fraction of my life. If I use it to age myself, it ages along with me. Things I truly leave behind I never retrieve, or even want to.

Yet occasionally, only at home in Sharon Springs, I live again in that childhood domain, where fantasy remains my possession. Not that I search for it; a mood like this must sneak up unawares. That incredible night last summer, as my friend and I sprawled against that hill that I used to call Strawberry Hill because of the gems that dot it every June, watched ashen clouds storm across the purple backdrop of the entire Mohawk Valley and the Adirondacks beyond. My friend commented that our prostration in the tall grass reminded him of a Wyeth painting, *Christina's World*. I took two giant steps, a flying leap and measured my length, belly up, in the grass.

"Eben's world."

© 1991 Houghton Mifflin Company. All rights reserved.

Faltering Muse

by David Levine

I've finished only one story in my life. One story and six four-line poems.
And as for those who would tell me that writing is never finished, only
abandoned, I would ask them not to diminish my meagre achievements
any further; I have finished one story and six four-line poems. As far as
the rest of my creative output is concerned, the old aphorism describes
it uncomfortably well: my writing is never finished. It is always abandoned. My notebooks are filled with page upon page of stillborn stories
and perished poems. And it's not for lack of ideas, either. I've always
forsaken my writing way before I hit a dry patch. No, in purely temporal
terms the stories and poems never get finished because whenever I have
the time to write, I haven't the enthusiasm. Perhaps "courage" would
be a better word. I can never work up the courage to write, and creativity is in large part a question of overcoming cowardice. Cowardice, not
fear; for in my experience the grit of creation is not so much something
to be dreaded as something to be avoided, something one "would rather
not have to deal with." The difference, say, between a chimera and a
cockroach. There are just so many threads to keep track of: whether all
the elements work together, whether they work individually, and
whether the way they work is appropriate. Are you letting your work
descend into chaos, or is it so much under your control that it seems
contrived? Are you allowing your content to dictate your form, or is that
just a coward's substitute for style anyhow? Is it original? If so, is it
good? If so, is it as good as your last one? Have you hammered your
audience over the head with meaning, or is it so subtle twelve critics
couldn't find it with a microscope? Do you even give a damn? Who cares
if it's well received? Who are you doing this for, anyhow? Yourself or
the audience?

Thankfully a great many of these questions can be ignored. I never
answer them; I just block them out. This summer, for instance, I had a
vague idea for a story: a notion of the characters involved, a sense of
what the crucial event would be, but no concept of beginning or end.
Just an idea that I wanted to explore, and that idea would dictate the
story to me. My degree of choice was infinite. I like working this way
because it gives me an impetus to finish: I want to find out how the
story ends. Also, whatever one produces this way is, if not good, at least
organic; the writing reflects the infinite progressions of correspondences
of thought. I work best as a slave to my Idea, all my energies devoted
to letting it go where it wants. By keeping such considerations as theme
and meaning, metaphor, plot, style, and audience at a remove, I avoid
the self-conscious paralysis they provoke. The mechanisms of fiction—

© 1991 Houghton Mifflin Company. All rights reserved.

theme, metaphor, et al.—turn up anyhow, but I only allow myself to become conscious of them *as mechanisms* once the groundwork has been laid, once the story has been drafted, for the manipulation of these elements is the business of the conscious mind. At the beginning the Idea must be allowed to do as it pleases; it is cosmic in its potential scope and encompasses a range of meanings and nuance far vaster than anything tight-fisted consciousness could offer. I only apply my conscious mind to the work, only worry about the theme and the form, once the idea has had its play. Creation should be, to use a prosaic simile, like trimming a hedge. Initially we let nature work at random. Not knowing where twigs and branches are going to sprout, we simply let the hedge grow. Once it has grown, though, we must trim it to keep it from proliferating out of control. Self-consciousness' place is analogous to the hedgeclippers'—we use it to give our creation a definite shape and to keep it from growing out of control, for if it does, neither the artist's nor the audience's mind will be able to discern it.

Grand theory. I didn't finish the story anyhow. The problem is, the more aware you are of those questions, the more menacingly they loom before you at the start of every project. I ignore the questions intrinsic to the creative process, wondering if I'm being too subtle, if my theme is apparent and such. But the external ones, pointless questions borne of extreme self-consciousness, stop me cold. What if I hit a dry spot? What if I don't finish this story? Why should I? I never have before. Isn't what we call "literary style" just an author's entrenched bad habits? Why even bother with "working around a theme?" Why not just say what it is we have to say in three or four lines and be done with it? Of course, I stop writing way before I run out of ideas; imagine how I'd deal with *that*. But what all these questions, what all this self-imposed uncertainty represents is the most common of worries: fear of failure.

I cope with the fear by abandoning work before it can fail (or for that matter succeed). Others complete their endeavors but still succumb to fear. My friend Antonio is a concert fortepianist. An earlier, smaller, and far less resonant version of the modern piano, the fortepiano was in use during the eighteenth and early nineteenth centuries and is enjoying a revival of sorts due to the "period-instruments" craze. I assumed, then, that Antonio chose to be a fortepianist because he believes deeply, as many do, that it is a violation of Mozart or Beethoven's art to play their music on a modern piano, as that is not the instrument for which their works were composed. It doesn't matter if he limits his own artistic options, just so long as he remains true to one piece. On the other hand, as a concert pianist who prefers the Steinway Grand once said to me, "If Beethoven could have gotten his hands on a modern piano, don't you think he would have used it?" This in mind, I asked Antonio one day why he had chosen the far less versatile fortepiano over

© 1991 Houghton Mifflin Company. All rights reserved.

the piano. "Oh, no," he replied, "I would never have made it on a modern piano. I haven't got that kind of talent."

Last summer I attended a performance of Beethoven's Sixth ("Pastorale") and Eighth symphonies conducted by Roger Norrington, played by his London Classical Players. He and his orchestra are period-instrument specialists, their approach to classical music being that in order to remain faithful to a composer's intent, one must recreate the performance practices and technique of the age in which the piece was written. The movement came into being in response to the hitherto unquestioned practice of playing all music, from baroque to contemporary, on modern instruments. Modern metal flutes, for example, have a wider octaval range and a different tone than the wooden flutes of Bach's time. Even old, old instruments, say the Stradivarius violin, have endured so much preservational maintenance over the centuries that their tone, while undeniably beautiful, is not the same as it was when they were crafted. Orchestras have on the whole grown, and contrary to what one may have seen in *Amadeus,* the position of conductor didn't even exist in Mozart's time. Indeed, the notion of using a noninstrumentalist to lead the orchestra didn't come into existence until early in the nineteenth century. Prior to that, orchestras were usually led by the first violinist or harpsichordist. Bearing this in mind, the period-performance school argues that modern performances of pre-Romantic music betray the composers' intentions. The sounds of which they conceived are not those which modern instruments produce, hence the emphasis on "authenticity."

But by Beethoven's time the orchestral instruments in use were nearly the same as those we use today, and conductors were being used, so it struck me as odd that the publicity for this concert, and there was much of it, insisted on the historical accuracy of this performance. Granted, there would be some differences, the most obvious being a much thinner tone owing, among other things, to the use of gut strings, less vibrato, and thinner bows in the string section. But these differences are not really apparent to the layman. Indeed, unless all the parts had been rescored for trombone it would be difficult not to be historically accurate as, save for orchestral size, there is very little for most people to distinguish between modern and period performances of Beethoven's orchestral works. (Norrington has since worked his way through the repertoire of Romantic works and has got as far as Wagner, the emphasis on "historical accuracy" becoming increasingly meaningless the closer Norrington creeps toward the twentieth century. But the emphasis has nonetheless been retained, if only to give otherwise mediocre performances a highly profitable pedigree.) Really, I couldn't understand why a period-performance orchestra would even bother with Beethoven.

Tempo. Tempo, tempo, tempo. As it turns out there is one difference: Beethoven was among the first to use metronome markings in his scores, and for some reason on which experts have yet to agree, they

© 1991 Houghton Mifflin Company. All rights reserved.

seem to dictate that the music be played unnaturally fast. Some musicologists mired, Norrington might say, in their own modernity suggest that as Beethoven was using one of the first metronomes, his speeds were set differently than they are today. Other, less sympathetic scholars suggest that Beethoven was too deaf to realize his metronome was broken. Norrington rejects both possibilities. The score is precisely as Beethoven intended it, and we should be loyal to his conception of the piece.

So in the name of historical accuracy Norrington tore through two of Beethoven's cheerier orchestral works, neither of which has slow movements anyhow (the slowest is marked *andante molto mosso,* which translates as "very agitated moderate speed"), as I sat there wondering why I hadn't stayed at home, put on some Beethoven LPs at 78 rpm, achieved the same effect, and saved twenty dollars. I do not here denigrate Norrington's aesthetic sensibilities, for, as far as I was concerned, he afforded us no opportunity to discern them. The music went by so fast there wasn't any room for depth or subtlety of feeling on his part. Indeed, it was the only performance of Beethoven I've ever heard that could be properly characterized as "perky."

Somewhat disconcerted, I went home and listened to a glorious recording of the late Wilhelm Furtwängler conducting his Berlin Philharmonic in a live performance of Beethoven's Fifth and "Pastorale" symphonies. The Fifth is in a minor key and, gratefully, has a slow movement. Of course, Furtwängler conducted in the days before efficiency experts, one of whom, when asked by a classical radio station a few years back how best to improve their ratings, advised, "Don't play the slow parts." Fast, noisy movements require less concentration on the part of the modern listener than slow ones, just as the sound of birds chirping in the fields in G major is far easier to cope with than fate slamming down your door in C minor. Undeniably the "Pastorale" and the Eighth are beautiful, but they are also among the most accessible of Beethoven's symphonies. All their profundity, however, was lost in Norrington's performance.

And maybe, on some level unknown to himself, that was the way he wanted it. A conductor's artistic task could be defined as the evocation through interpretation of the soul of a piece of music. It is the choices the conductor must face—how long to pull out notes, the relative volumes to assign the different instrumental sections, the tempo of a piece and the transformations of this tempo—which make him an artist. These decisions are potentially ruinous, but they are ultimately what animate creativity. That which does not involve the risk of choice is not art. By the time you've finished paring down your orchestra to period size, replacing your instruments and prostrating yourself before tempo markings, there is no longer any room for interpretation. If we resign ourselves to mere recreation, no initiative is involved, and what we have before us is an academic museum piece rather than art. Whereas Antonio coped with his fear of failure by scaling down the range of

© 1991 Houghton Mifflin Company. All rights reserved.

decisions he could make, the only choice Norrington made was to avoid making choices. Orchestral music needs a conductor for its greatness to be realized. In his very risky and personal interpretations, Furtwängler made Beethoven's art tangible and in so doing proved himself an artist. Norrington did nothing for Beethoven or himself. He dealt with artistic uncertainty by rejecting artistry.

His audience loved it. They were still giving him a standing ovation when I left. In fact, they probably appreciated him more unquestioningly than any audience Furtwängler ever played to because Norrington placed no demands on them. Even those who appreciate Furtwängler eventually wonder about some of his choices, whether he doesn't go too far, for instance, in his stretching of tempi. His choices work, but mightn't he be taking too many liberties with the score? No such questions can be asked of Norrington, for he has Historical Accuracy on his side. But that accuracy constrains his creativity; although art is nurtured by history, it must never be bound by it. Furtwängler confronted his audience with his decisions. He made his choices, answered the self-conscious questions which attend these choices, and threw the questions back at the audience. It is now we who must ask "Was he too obvious? Was this overdone?" And the audience should be faced with these questions, for it gave rise to them. The artist indulges in this endless, self-conscious interrogation because he wonders if the choices he has made will lead him to failure. The fear of failure arises because we are human beings endowed with the consciousness that there is a world which does not necessarily agree with, and often opposes, our views. The fount of creative uncertainty is the artist's awareness of an audience.

I have four of my vaguely Dadaist assemblages in my room. When someone asks me what they are I don't call them "sculptures," but "just things I put together." I'd like to call them "sculptures," but if I do they must bear the weight of their own tradition. And in whose eyes must they bear this weight? The audience's, the Audience which quickly becomes the Critic if it sniffs pride. If I say, "Just something I put together," then I consider it negligible, and if the artist considers his work negligible, the audience will neglect it. But when there is pride to be deflated, then Jekyll defers to Hyde and the Critic bares his fangs. Hell, why do you think I just picked Norrington apart? True, on principle I have no respect for his approach, but I wouldn't have been half so self-righteous if he hadn't been so obviously pleased with himself. I'm proud of my work, too; I just don't let anyone know it. I don't precisely dislike the audience; if art is to make a statement, someone must be there to listen. It's just that the audience makes the actual utterance a lot more difficult.

Ah, how I long for the days of the Dogs! The Dogs of Jazz came into being one night when my friends and I were doing some really awful improv in my room. Me on flute, Sandy on violin, Peabo on bass. Each of us was playing in a different key, none of us on the same beat.

© 1991 Houghton Mifflin Company. All rights reserved.

Cacophony reigned. But people kept stopping by the room and saying, "That's great, man. So avant-garde." Now while I don't subscribe to the view that a two-year-old could've painted Jackson Pollock's paintings, I do believe he could fool a few people. This in mind, we booked ourselves at a coffee house, got a drummer, an electric guitarist, and a singer to scream Top-40 lyrics over whatever white noise we happened to be producing, rehearsed once, and played an evening of "poststructuralist bebop" for an audience of about sixty. We alternated between actually playing "songs" (at least that's what we called them; we can't play so they probably all sounded alike) and doing beat-style readings of D. H. Lawrence, Derrida, and a truly awful poem inspired by Ginsberg's *Howl*. We were just doing this for our own amusement; the audience could go to hell. Anyone philistine enough to take us seriously deserved to be annoyed.

Some people didn't take us seriously. Most did. Of those who did, some didn't like us. Most did. One guy even went so far as to come up after the show and tell us that that was the way music should be played. And we weren't contemptuous; we were flattered. Flattered and a bit stunned. After a full hour and a half of standing in a cramped room, sitting in uncomfortable chairs or even on the floor and listening to our discordant Dog music, they certainly weren't supposed to dig us. Three weeks later we were asked to play a benefit for the campus anarchist magazine. Makes sense, I suppose. By this time, though, people had heard about us and expected to be pleased by our "sound," whatever that was. We tried to keep things loose, really we did, but the mingled flattery and pressure of an expectant audience made us far more concerned this time with what we would do and how we would do it. We couldn't tell the audience to fuck off because we'd done that the first time and they like how we said it. None of us really enjoyed playing that concert because none of us wanted to have to please anyone. But they had appropriated us, and what were we to do?

The presence of an audience creates uncertainty because it offers the artist the pernicious option of taking another person's point of view. When the writer rewrites, the composer rescores, the painter modifies, what is he doing but putting himself in the audience's shoes? "How would this look to me if I hadn't sculpted it? How does it really look?" Our modifications are answers to all those self-conscious questions we ask ourselves. By asking these questions we try to anticipate the Audience/Critic's perspective, and we do so because we know, even when we think we've succeeded, there is still the audience to cry us down and tell us we have failed. That is the effect of an audience's presence, and most of us haven't the confidence to ignore the extra perspective they provide. For there is always the violent whirlpool of uncertainty, the knowledge that our judgment is eminently fallible.

But the extra perspective is a damned burden because it makes us more self-conscious than we were to start with. The Dogs tried to fend

© 1991 Houghton Mifflin Company. All rights reserved.

off the audience's point of view by offending it. By ignoring their wants we isolated ourselves, made our "art" (our trash, whatever) completely *pour soi*. We didn't care what they thought, we didn't even know what they thought, hence no self-consciousness. Until they approved of us. By doing so they showed themselves to be commiserators, and given a chance to see ourselves through their eyes, to "broaden our perspective" (and thereby our confusion), we couldn't refuse. Antonio, by diminishing the range of his choices, lessened the number of questions the Audience/Critic could ask of him and thus the number of questions he had to ask of himself. Norrington just gave the audience what it wanted: major-key, prepackaged, supposedly highbrow performances. He pacified their voice but in so doing cheated himself. Most of us have to choose: pacify the crowd or satisfy the muse.

Furtwängler, like all great artists, chose the muse and managed, somehow. He must have asked the questions, certainly put himself in the audience's shoes, struggled with the creeping paralysis of self-consciousness. Yet he did not compromise himself. And the reason, the answer to the whole problem is simple. It's what I mentioned at the start, before I dug up all this unnecessary dirt: courage. Courage, which is of equal parts ego and conviction. Ego, so that the artist can ultimately prefer his own opinion to that of the audience, and conviction to back up that preference. We must not ignore the audience's judgment, but neither must we obey it. The trick is ultimately in the stance the creator assumes towards the world of spectators, for while uncertainty arises from self-consciousness, self-consciousness does not arise from the self; it arises from borrowing the perspective of another.

© 1991 Houghton Mifflin Company. All rights reserved.

Having Things

by Eve Pearlman

I worry about myself and things because I can't seem to own them, to make them mine in quite the way I imagine I'm supposed to. I live with a woman who really seems to possess the objects she gathers around her. Rebecca covers her walls with posters and postcards. She has jewelry and scissors and white correction fluid. Above her mantle she has hung two white pieces of tissue paper that a neighbor block-printed with dark purple flowers. She keeps things that are part of her past, like a field hockey stick, and stuff she uses every day. Sometimes when I'm in her room I feel flawed because I don't seem to accumulate things and take care of them. I feel like I'm missing some important aesthetic sense.

Recently, after suffering from a nasty canker sore inside my lower lip for almost a week, I asked Rebecca if she had something that could help me. I had just eaten tomatoes. Tomatoes irritate canker sores, they're very acidic. She rummaged in a small pink nylon bag filled with little containers and tubes—I guess she kept makeup in that one. In a little green bag about the same size as the pink one, she found some Kanka, which I discovered is a brown liquid stored in a tiny bottle. I dabbed the sore with the little fuzzy applicator and it numbed the irritated area in my mouth. She'd saved it, it hadn't leaked out on the bottom of some bag or been lost in her car or smashed on the floor of her room.

There are things like Kanka which are functional and helpful. People save them, not because they hold great sentimental value but because they're practical. But there is something else, something more confusing, that people do with objects; they put a lot of sentimental energy into them. I guess maybe some people feel that an actual object, say, like their bowling ball, means something in and of itself—that the object, the physical form, is somehow significant. But mostly it seems that we like things because they remind us of people or places or times. The object doesn't contain the memory, but it's tangible, a solid reminder that bridges the spaces between our memories and our present.

The summer after my seventh grade year in school I went to camp. I was happy and safe and did what kids are expected to do at camp. I ran and swam in the sun, I gossiped at night in the cabin, I climbed up a big hill, and I sang camp songs and watched people. And I met people. They were mostly from New York, and there were lots of promises to write. And we wrote, and I saved the letters and a purple grape eraser that Greg gave me, and a sweater that I traded with Samantha. I believed in the objects until the following fall when I confronted them as I cleaned out my room. As I tried to decide if I should keep them, it became clear to me that they didn't matter and that I didn't need them.

© 1991 Houghton Mifflin Company. All rights reserved.

This made me feel deficient because I had read enough books to be aware of the pattern where a lover gives a glove, or a note, or some other object, and it is treasured in a secret drawer. It didn't feel important to save the letters, the eraser, and the sweater, and they cluttered my closet. Those friends from camp gradually became pieces of my past. I had let them affect me, be with me that summer in the only way that I imagine it possible to possess people. Our separate feelings, ideas, and selves were modified and merged as we talked, judged, and defined ourselves and the people around us. But I couldn't possess them into the future. I've imagined, as I've watched the mystery of ownership around me, that relationships with things are like those with people. Or maybe I just assume they are because relationships with people are the only kind I think I know how to have. But I can't quite seem to equate feelings for people—who talk, respond, and move—with feelings for things.

I made resolutions this summer to try to keep the things I had around me, hold them there, because I was frustrated by the trail of things I'd lost. I wanted to try to possess. In June, ostensibly because I was turning nineteen, but mostly because they didn't want me borrowing the car, my mother and father bought me a new red mountain bike, an amazing eighteen-gear machine. They bought it with their money especially for me. Riding it, I could stop and get on and off without banging my crotch or scraping a pedal on the ground. It was different from all the inherited bikes of my childhood. It fit me, it was for me.

I was a little apprehensive at first, apprehensive about identifying with ownership. It seemed strange to take proud responsibility for owning something that anyone could own if they had the cash to buy it. Cash, money, and the worth of material possessions outside my own head are an issue that I have been trying to avoid floating toward, but here it is. There is a sensible reason to take care of things: money. Apparently money makes some objects more valuable than others because it takes more money to get them. Even so, I have trouble believing. I can't, unless I twist myself into a strange, impoverished situation and refuse to ask for help, or if the world as we know it were to crumble. It seems I'll always have the things that I need to live, like food and warm clothes and a place with a bed in it. Other things, tools and appliances that I have or want, float at a distance from the necessities.

It isn't that I'm excessively rich, because I'm not. There are limits to my family's resources. It's just that the limits are far enough away that I live quite comfortably without pushing them. I've never had to carefully match amounts of money with hard objects. The relationship between them—that money allows you to have certain things and not others—hasn't been part of my reality. It isn't that I haven't worked, but I don't match an hour of work to the experience of a five dollar movie or meal; they're incongruent. I spend far more than I ever make, and I almost always spend on stuff that I don't need. I did buy forty

© 1991 Houghton Mifflin Company. All rights reserved.

"necessary" rolls of toilet paper for my house recently, though we'd somehow managed without it for a week. My parents complain sometimes that I don't make good concrete links between money and things. They do, or, rather, they choose to because it makes money and work and the order they live by solid, not abstract. For me, the college tuition they pay is another difficult concept to grasp because I can't imagine how the layers and layers of thousands translate into the moments of my day and the thoughts in my head at this university. Cost and need, real need, aren't part of my reality.

It seems silly to take pride in owning a thing that anyone with money could go into a store and buy, though I'm stuck with the same image we're all taught—the one of a little kid who works hard, saves his (and it is always a "he" in the stories) allowance, and buys something big for himself. Maybe there's a reason for pride there, but the pride isn't in the object. It's in the determination and the control it took to save and not in the bought Bigwheel.

My red bike became the symbol of a lot of things quickly. It was my independence. It was my exercise—it changed the shape of my thighs and calves. It changed the shape and size of the little city I'd lived in all my life. I could go to the nearest town, eight miles away up the canyon, in a few hours. I could go visit friends, rent movies, explore different streets by myself any time I wanted. The bike didn't do these things for me, I did them using my bike as a tool. But because the bike was an enabler, because it allowed me to change my world limits, I tended to credit it with the victories of my new movements. My bike does not, of course, deserve the credit. I think my affection was misplaced affection for myself.

My bike became a focus for a lot of energy. It was a big thing, and I thought that by owning and caring for it I'd learn to possess things. But there was another undercurrent. I wanted to try to have what I imagined to be the right kind of relationship, something that mirrored the affection and loyalty that other people, like Rebecca, seem to have for their things. I focused careful attention on the affection people have for their cars: I watched them talk to, name, and attribute gender to their dumpy old Chevys and their shiny new Subarus. I was perpetually frightened that my bike would get stolen or disappear from my life.

I have traced the possible beginnings of this fear to a family trip across the country when I was little. On long trips my brothers and I would store candy in the ashtrays. Somehow, during a long Nebraska afternoon, I bobbled the removable ashtray in my hands as I was getting out a butterscotch, and the ashtray went out the window. The feeling I had then, the "Oh no, it's gone," is very much like the feeling I still get when I lose or break something that I am trying to make part of me, like the scarf around my neck or the thick wool socks on my feet. It is when these things pass that barrier, when they are left in the gym or lent to someone, when they pass out of the loose orbit of stuff that is

© 1991 Houghton Mifflin Company. All rights reserved.

mine and disappear into the wide space of things that are not mine, that I remember the bobble of the ashtray and the knock against the window as it went out. It feels like that, with the added "Oh well" from repetition.

The part of this ashtray episode that has probably affected my conception of things most is the reaction of my family. They were amused. And though I do remember my dad telling me later how much it had cost to buy a new one, the price didn't touch me, the ashtray was replaceable—it was a piece of plastic. We didn't need it and it didn't really matter.

Our family friends and relatives always complained that my parents spoiled us. When I lost my new winter jacket in ninth grade, they bought me another one. When my radio fell down the stairs, I got a new one a few months later. It often happened like that. Other times my mom would make deals with me for new things. I'd wash the windows or iron tablecloths for money, but I don't think it ever made much sense to any of us. I lived in their house and ate their food. The great majority of the money, except the few dollars I made baby-sitting, came from them. I did so little, they gave me so much. How could I possibly figure a relationship between work and time and things? The earliest vivid memory I have of my father is of him telling me never to cry over things, only people. "We don't cry over things in this family," he said. "Things can be replaced." And they can. But somewhere I missed some distinction between crying and simply taking care.

Through my attention to my bike this summer I was trying to teach myself this distinction. I wanted to teach myself to care, but I couldn't seem to find a new category of feeling. There are people, and somewhere else, but not inside me, there must be a place, a way to deal with the keeping of things. I was trying, nonetheless, to prepare for the time, two or three years away, when I would be supporting myself and things would have concrete financial meanings, when I would have to take the time to make the money to have things. This summer I constantly reminded myself that I needed my bike, which I actually didn't, but I tried to reinforce the idea that I wasn't going to get another, and I wasn't going to get a car.

I kept my bike in my room with me while I slept. If I did leave it on the porch when I stopped home on my break from work, I'd run out and check it a few times during lunch. Even when I locked it outside during a movie or a dinner, I'd be happy and relieved to see it still there when I got back. I depended on it, or pretended I did, to get through the days, but I wasn't certain that I had a right to it. It seemed like too good a thing, too special a thing to own a whole bike that was mine, that fit me, that worked. It felt strange that I cared for it, rode it, and had the full use of it.

This fall it got stolen. I came out from class one day and it was gone. My kryptonite lock was lying on the ground, still locked around the pole,

© 1991 Houghton Mifflin Company. All rights reserved.

but my bike was gone. I thought maybe Doug, who I'd given the second key to for safekeeping, had borrowed it and left the lock so I'd know that only he could have taken it. As I walked to work, away from the spot where my bike wasn't, I felt a little relief nudging around inside me. If my bike had been stolen, I wouldn't have to worry, to cling to it, to put energy into making sure that it still existed in my possession. I could just walk. I liked the rhythm of my feet on the grass, slower and somehow more manageable.

I called Doug when I got to work. He hadn't borrowed my bike. I panicked, then I figured. I figured I had locked the lock around the pole but failed to loop it through the bike's frame. The pleasant relief was gone and I felt very stupid, inept. I had invested a lot of energy into keeping that bike. It had carried me in a separate world, but I still couldn't seem to own things into the future. I was angry at myself, and I felt inadequate. I kept asking myself, again and again, those questions we ask when we do something unfathomably stupid: what is wrong with me? what is wrong?

Public Safety came and took the report. I called my parents to get the bike's serial number. My dad said, "Don't panic, it's just a thing." My mom got worried during the summer that the bike would get stolen and I'd freak. She'd warned me not to make it mean so much, to remember that it was a replaceable thing. This was very confusing because I was trying to train myself to think of it as very important and irreplaceable. I refused to admit that it was just a bike and let it be symbolic of a lot of things. Owning a bike meant that I had a chance of controlling my environment, a chance at creating a useful orbit of "my" things around me.

My brother used to be one of the three kids in my family, but now, at twenty-three, he lives in a different city and has a job and an apartment. He's starting to do things that adults do. I remember talking to him from my dorm room one day during finals. He had just gone shopping and had bought a stainless steel cheese grater and a garlic press, and he was very pleased. They were objects he'd been needing for cooking. I had trouble getting excited, and that compelled me to notice that we were at distinctly different life stages. He was buying utensils; I was stealing spoons from the dining hall to eat instant soup. He's continued doing it, buying things to be part of the new life he is building for himself. He is beginning as a new family. When my parents visit him he cooks dinner for them in his home with his things. They might watch a movie with him too, he just bought a VCR. When my mom came to visit me, we went out to eat and she slept on sheets and under a blanket that she had bought.

But she and my father had bought the bike for me. I guess the difference between it and my sheets is that I claimed responsibility for it. It was mine. I paid for its repairs—this is money again, but it is money without an origin—and I used it to go places and see people that were

© 1991 Houghton Mifflin Company. All rights reserved.

separate from my parents. Mostly, though, I think the important difference was that I claimed it. It was my problem and my joy.

This summer, when I told people that I loved my bike, they'd ask what sex it was. Or, sometimes, if they didn't volunteer the question I'd ask them. It really bothered me that I couldn't seem to label my bike male or female. I couldn't even pick a name. I thought about it, hoped that instinct would hit me and I would know, but I didn't. It was a bike, a thing, an object. Things are not men and women. Animals can be male and female, but people are women and men, and these words say a lot about the experience and the identity and the ideas of the people. Gender exists for people.

And yet I wanted my bike to have a gender because I wanted it to be able to reciprocate in the relationship that I was trying to have with it. I wanted it to fit into a human category. Mostly, though, I worried about it getting stolen and was excited every time it was in the same place where I'd left it because that was all it could do. It couldn't talk, it couldn't think. It could ride well, but I mostly took that for granted. All it could do was exist, and even its existence wasn't particularly dynamic. It existed because someone had built it, had made the parts. It didn't exist specifically for me. I was prepared to respond to it the way I respond to people, but getting angry at it when the gearshift was slightly off isn't like confronting a person. Bikes don't shape reality with you.

I have been trying, over and over, to compare relationships with things to relationships with people, but it won't work. Objects aren't important like people. Most objects belong in the category of useful and functional things, like Rebecca's Kanka. Things clutter around people. They bang into each other in orbit. They block vision to other things, like food and clothing that are really useful, and to selves which are really interesting. I think my biggest problem is with things I don't need because when I don't need them, it seems silly to exert energy making sure they stay put around me. Things are just things. They might be useful, they might be pretty, but those aren't reasons to care for them particularly.

Rebecca holds onto things and clings to beautiful objects for a bunch of reasons. They are part of her outward identity. What is she trying to say about herself with those things? Is it that she thinks her good taste, or taste, period, is somehow indicative of her own beauty? I'm not so sure. I think Rebecca, and she knows this, uses things as a barrier between herself and the rest of us, the people outside. They protect her, but also I think she loves herself through those things; I think she loves her own ability to love them. I pretend to possess people in the same way Rebecca pretends to possess things. We each cling, to give ourselves a sense of not being alone.

My bike was found, dumped behind some fraternity by a scared thief. I was excited to get it back. Excited by the adventure of making a

© 1991 Houghton Mifflin Company. All rights reserved.

statement at the police station and retelling the story later. And I was glad. I could make it from home to class quickly. I could ride with my friends, clicking through the gears across campus, missing the careful tread of my feet on the grass. My property was back. But it's different now. I pay less attention to it—I leave it in the hallway instead of in my room.

© 1991 Houghton Mifflin Company. All rights reserved.

Guns

by Jacques Whitecloud

When I was sixteen the two things I missed most were bacon and guns. Leaning liberally to the left, I was antivivisection, and eating bacon would mean I condoned the murder of an innocent pig; being a pacifist ruled out liking guns because they're usually a pretty important part of armed conflicts today. But if imitation bacon bits never really made a good BLT, reading newsprint magazines about the need for world peace through anarcho-communism wasn't even close to watching a good action movie and wondering what it would be like to blaze some nameless foe down with an Uzi while bullets went zinging all around (and never through) me.

Now I think I should set some things straight. I'm a college student with clean criminal and psychological records. My last real fight was in second grade. I feel a love for America because it's home, and I think I would risk my life defending it only if someone were trying to break in. I am no flag-waving, lowbrow psychotic, but I like guns; I've *pretended* not to, *told* myself not to, but never could. Last year during orientation week I stopped by a dorm room in my hall and introduced myself. There were four other men in the room, hailing from New York farming towns, Pittsburgh, and Boston; conversation suffered a few false starts, and then guns came up, and we all had something to say about firearms from the Civil War to Vietnam. To hell with football, guns are the national male pastime and have been since the beginning. Maybe it's not too likely that you'll have to drive out the British anymore, but guns are still so important to congressmen and American men in general that we have a constitutional right to them. Is there a constitutional right to football? Of course not. Guns are what bind American men together. Maybe every male can't rattle off rates of fire and relative stopping power of various rounds, but I think most are at least familiar with terms like .45 auto, M-16, and 9 mm. I've always thought that men who lobby for gun control sound more convincing than women; you have to have loved something to *really* hate it.

Guns in themselves make poor obsessions, though maybe for reasons which make being obsessed with them the only way of liking them at all. They're limited in their usefulness, basically only good for killing things; pistols could make good paperweights, or maybe hammers, though the latter use only occurs to people after they've run out of ammo. Other faults include high cost and unattractiveness—even for a weapon they're

87

© 1991 Houghton Mifflin Company. All rights reserved.

very plain. But men can see past all this. Guns can do wrong, sure, but they also can do magic, if you believe in them.

I've never really had the urge to write a paper about my penis; hence (read that as a very rational "hence") when I sat down to write this I didn't give much credence to the gun-as-phallic-symbol theory. But a lot about guns doesn't mesh with the "hence" part of the male mind; a lot about guns lies under the mud beneath. Men, you see, basically are infatuated with guns to different degrees. Some, like me, have a junior high crush on guns—I've never even fired one—and have to be content with fantasy. Others take it quite a bit further—consider Patrick Purdy, who used a California schoolyard for a shooting gallery last January. Guns have a lot going for them: old westerns and new action movies assure a man that a gun will never let him down if he never lets it go; it'll always be at his side, there when he needs it, quiet and out of the way when he doesn't; it can even protect him from bullies, like Mom used to. And of course guns make a man a *man*, without having to worry about "measuring up"—a constant worry in another, more anxiety-ridden proving ground of masculinity.

Sounds like what many men might consider the ideal woman. There does seem to be an attraction to combinations of females and firearms; *Soldier of Fortune* magazine sells the Girls with Guns series of video-tapes (excerpt from the ad, beneath the big-haired woman in a bikini: "see Tami firing the Mac-10, Mini-14, and AK-47!"), and occasionally a porno magazine will run a pictorial of a naked woman straddling an M-60 or the heavy gun on a tank. Consider the gun as the perfect woman and it's easier to understand the market for bumperstickers which say things like, "My wife, yes; my dog, maybe; my gun, *never.*" And what a man they make you: consider who's known for their piece over their personalities. Mel Gibson. John Wayne. Stallone. *Clint.* And of course there's Lee Harvey Oswald, the Son of Sam, and John Hinckley, Jr. If a gun doesn't boost your testosterone level to astro-nomically aggressive, hairy levels, it at least garners respect. Things like, say, philanthropy or effective communication skills fall behind guns on the Real Manhood barometer because they don't offer to any man, great or small, smart or dumb, the power to instantly and assuredly ripple history in some great or small way—but definitely a *manly* way. I think the stereotype of gun-loving and gun-carrying men (it's impor-tant to distinguish the lovers from those who carry guns to protect themselves from the lovers) being sexist, misogynistic people has quite a few grains of truth in it; for some reason they feel their manhood is being questioned every day, and if they can't prove it by shooting some-one, they can at least denigrate women and widen the gender gap. A gun in the hand becomes virility, strength, and aggression because a gun in the hand cancels virility, strength, and aggression, and cancels them romantically, with a coughed-out fireball and a thunderclap. What could be better?

© 1991 Houghton Mifflin Company. All rights reserved.

A lot, I think some men would say. My mother was once planting poppies in front of our house, and my Uncle Henry got very upset. It turned out that in WWII he had to lie perfectly motionless in a field of poppies for several hours; if he moved, the flowers moved, and the enemy troops which were patrolling the field for Allied soldiers on their bellies would know where to shoot. Uncle had his gun with him, but it didn't help. Guns promise a lot, and I guess that if you haven't experienced them in earnest, it's easy to believe them.

Instant manhood seems too good to be true, and to see goodness beyond truth means the wonderful freedom of throwing logic out the window. The legally blind are denied firearms, but firearms induce a certain blindness in their owners. I think the owner of the bumpersticker would have to admit that his dog and maybe even his wife are better to have around than his gun; his dog won't blow a hole in him accidentally, and his wife or son or father won't blow a hole in him or themselves if there's no gun around. He'd especially have to admit it if you broke into his house at night and held his gun to his head. But men can cloud their eyes to all this; love of guns clings behind reason in imagination, like a locust's husk to bark. Men, even educated, professional men, can like or love guns because they learn to before they can reason that *kill* means *killed,* and *killed* means *dead.* American boys learn to love guns, Mom, and Dad at the same early age; though I haven't liked my parents at times, I've never not liked guns. I suppose that I've daydreamed about myself in situations involving firearms or one sort or another more than anything else, since the other contender for dreamtime, sex, didn't become interesting until comparatively recently. And I'll venture to say that a lot of American male childhood involves gun play: there's cops and robbers, there's cowboys and Indians, there's army—little boys and guns. When I was six or seven I had a blue plastic M-16, just like the ones our boys had carried in Vietnam two years earlier. It rattled when you pumped the trigger, and I had a quiet epiphany the day I figured out that it wasn't the noise but the bullets that killed people. My father —who avoided Vietnam—loved fighter planes; his father had been a paratrooper-medic in WWII, and he must have told Dad some really great stories of dogfights (N.B.: Grampa would've *watched*) because Dad sure loved the model planes he built with my older sister. Dad was never very much into guns, though he owns one—maybe some other kids' dads came back to his hometown, maybe in boxes—but Dad didn't grow up with peace and TV, where guns don't kill people; they kill drug dealers or maniacs or other scum, and the scum always die very neatly, and neatly the next scene pushes them away. Killed by gunfire—my friend who was killed in a car accident somehow seems more dead than the one who shot himself. Death by shooting isn't really death, but romance.

Maybe guns would remain a boyhood fixation if, like magic dragons, boys couldn't grow into them. There are men who want fully automatic weapons with armor-piercing bullets to shoot at human silhouettes, "for

© 1991 Houghton Mifflin Company. All rights reserved.

recreation"—damn right, instead of blue plastic you can have the real thing. There are college students who can't fit their heads into the lasertag equipment (it's intended for children) they play with, who buy electric waterguns for use around the dorm. The gun is stuck in the male mentality by the glittery glue of boyhood's imagination. Guns are magic. Men who Are All They Can Be carry guns. Guns turn anyplace into a testicular zone where men do manly things like "going down going for it," as in *Extreme Prejudice*; stoically stitching up their own wounds, as in *First Blood*; and letting out throaty, manly screams when they get their calves blown off, as in *Platoon*. Some things, like the picture I saw of a hunter who has two black pits where his eyes had been before buckshot ripped them from his skull after he dropped his gun, make my enthusiasm for firearms dwindle a little. But only a little, and only for a little while. *I* would do the shooting; *I* wouldn't get shot.

What about women? Why don't they want in on the fun? Why didn't any of them buy the electric water Uzis and the lasertag stuff? There's a time in childhood when girls and boys alike point index fingers and say, "POW POW POW . . ." and boys play house and dolls with the girls. But before long those are boy-games and girl-games. And girls can become women and be CEOs, construction workers, even All They Can Be in the army, but guns are still a man-game. Whether or not women wish they could play I don't know. Women don't grow into guns like men do—the women I know today, on the rare occasions they pretend to have guns, say, "POW!" or maybe "Pewshh!" and cock their thumbs and shoot through their index fingers. Boys become men and learn to make a throaty rumble, and hold an invisible and large pistol grip in their hand, and work an invisible pump action, and sight down an invisible rifle barrel. Maybe some women are really into guns privately, but all my experience is to the contrary. I've been in conversations about guns with women around, and they always seem bored or thinking Mom's old rule: "games like that always end up in someone being hurt." The fact that Sigourney Weaver and female marines could blow things to bits with as much enthusiasm as the men only made *Aliens* seem more futuristic to me, as distant from day-to-day experience as the stories of frontierwomen shooting alongside the men or the photo I saw of Muslim women, dressed head to toe in black, learning to disassemble a rifle. It's true that Smith and Wesson is now making the Ladysmith revolver and targeting it (no pun intended) at female consumers, but its ads are centered on the fact that there are sick men who are bigger than they. You hear about American men and guns in stories about hunting, survivalist groups, and shootouts in the inner cities over money; you mostly hear about American women and guns after they've shot a rapist or an abusive husband or themselves. Unlike men, I think women would stay away from guns if they had the choice.

A love for guns—I can explain it, make fun of it, see it as irrational, but I can never leave it. A passerby in a car once *suggested* that he had

© 1991 Houghton Mifflin Company. All rights reserved.

a gun, and that I'd better give him five dollars. I thought I was going to wet my pants. On reflection, nonetheless, I didn't wish for a ban on civilian purchases of firearms, but for a pistol I could've pulled out of my pants to blow the guy's rear window out with. The guy would've sped away in his wounded car; I'd have a big, smoking thing in my hand. It would be glorious. "If you outlaw guns, only outlaws will have them"— that's the popular argument of gun lobbyists. Only outlaws will have all the fun, too; fantasies like mine would become a thing of the past. Guns are dangerous and overrated and frightening, but guns are cool. Hold a loaded one in your hand and it looks quietly innocent enough, but you can almost feel the potential energy chomping at the bit to go violently kinetic. If I were holding a gun in my hand right now, you would be paying very, very close attention to every word I said; try and name other hand-held objects which would have the same effect on everyone. And a note on their beauty, or lack of it: one of my roommates is a genius, and he spends his spare time designing firearms for law enforcement and civilian use; military weapons, he says, are unaesthetic. I disagree with Isaac; as I mentioned above, no gun is really beautiful in a classical sense. But a Mag-10 Roadblocker repeating shotgun can put a round through the back door of a station wagon and crack the engine block. If you follow Horatio Greenough's theory that form follows function in the beautiful, then guns are extremely aesthetic.

They may be reaching a temporary apex in their popularity soon, though. I read an interview in one of the less sleazy skin magazines with some historian in a nationally recognized history department (please pardon my vagueness—I never anticipated citing *Penthouse,* and details have slipped my mind) who has proposed that wars start with a sympathetic national conscience, one that is more and more accepting of things military and violent. A few pages later there were photographs of a woman posing nude with an Uzi. My apartmentmates and I sit around the kitchen table and talk about guns. Over the summer one hundred thousand people showed up to watch a platoon of marines storm a North Carolina beach. TV and movies now have a new hero, the Vietnam veteran back in the real world who is tortured by his experience in the hell of war but who can nonetheless crack hilarious jokes and get gorgeous women when he's not legally killing hundreds of villains without ever reloading his 9 mm. The old marine sergeant who ran Junior ROTC at my high school didn't need to read the article; he just said that the feeling was right for another war now, maybe in South America. If the historian is right, and there is a war right on the horizon, the best that we can hope for is a temporary lapse in the gun's popularity when enough uncles come home with poppy stories, and enough dads and sons come home in boxes.

© 1991 Houghton Mifflin Company. All rights reserved.